Supervision, Management, and Leadership

Supervision, Management, and Leadership

An Introduction to Building Community Benefit Organizations

JOHN E. TROPMAN

OXFORD
UNIVERSITY PRESS

Oxford University Press is a department of the University of Oxford. It furthers the University's objective of excellence in research, scholarship, and education by publishing worldwide. Oxford is a registered trade mark of Oxford University Press in the UK and certain other countries.

Published in the United States of America by Oxford University Press
198 Madison Avenue, New York, NY 10016, United States of America.

© Oxford University Press 2020

Library of Congress Cataloging-in-Publication Data
Names: Tropman, John E., author.
Title: Supervision, management, and leadership : an introduction to building community benefit organizations / John E. Tropman.
Description: New York : Oxford University Press, 2020. |
Includes bibliographical references and index.
Identifiers: LCCN 2019043011 (print) | LCCN 2019043012 (ebook) |
ISBN 9780190097875 (paperback) | ISBN 9780190097899 (epub)
Subjects: LCSH: Supervision. | Management. | Organizational sociology. |
Community development.
Classification: LCC HM1253 .T76 2020 (print) | LCC HM1253 (ebook) |
DDC 302.3/5—dc23
LC record available at https://lccn.loc.gov/2019043011
LC ebook record available at https://lccn.loc.gov/2019043012

9 8 7 6 5 4 3 2 1

Printed by Marquis, Canada

CONTENTS

PART 6 The Executive Edge: Honing and Sharpening

PREFACE

This book is a revised edition of *Supervision and Management in Nonprofits and Human Services*. There are several changes.

First, the scope of the book has been expanded. Earlier editions unpacked issues of supervisory and managerial leadership. This edition examines executive leadership as well. Second, this edition consolidates the concepts *nonprofit* and *human services* under the broader concept *community benefit organizations*. Community benefit organizations include organizations that have historically been called nonprofits, but they also encompass public organizations that work for community benefit and for-profit "triple bottom-line" organizations—those with an emphasis on people, profit, and planet. It was redesigned to serve as a refresher for those with significant experience, as well as an introduction for those who are just stepping into management. To this end, I have incorporated optional reflective practice exercises to help you identify where you are, how you want to develop, and how to start. Finally, this edition incorporates the insight of my colleagues and reflects the updates and improvements generally expected of a revision.

Our fundamental question remains the same: whether and how community benefit organizations can succeed in their missions—that is whether, and how, they can achieve both outcomes (results) and outputs (activities). High-performing systems are efficient (doing things right), are effective (doing the right thing), work from evidence, and make a lasting impact. If the organization is a kind of system, how can we tell whether it is high-performing, or not, and how can we start where we are to move our organizations toward optimal performance?

I hope this volume will help executives, managers, and supervisors develop *managerial and leadership competence*—knowledge and skills—that help them avoid inflicting on their staff and clients the ways they were once (mis)managed and (mis)led and will help them develop and motivate teams, optimize systems, and lead themselves and others in ways that transform their organizations.

John Tropman

Ann Arbor, MI, Glen Arbor, MI

ACKNOWLEDGMENTS

Every product or service is a collective effort. It is as true for books as anything else. There are formal and informal connections, and many people are involved in the outcome.

My wife, Penny, is a constant source of discussion and evaluation of all my work. My children, Sarah, Jessica, and Matthew, and my grandchildren Jared, Evelyn, the twins Dan and Ethan, and Charlotte continually provide me with fresh perspectives—ranging from angry coach-managers to hostile dance instructors. (If being the personal victim of bad supervisors, managers, and executives isn't hard enough, watching your children and grandchildren experience similar incompetence is even more troubling.) Whenever people supervise, manage, or act in an executive capacity many do it poorly. "Bad bosses" abound.

As I write this revision, many people who have influenced me over the years come to mind. My father, Elmer J. Tropman, was such a maestro that his work as executive director of the Council of Social Agencies in Buffalo and the Health and Welfare Planning Association in Pittsburgh came to be known as The Tropman Touch. He could bring disparate groups together for the overall common good. He was truly, to borrow Robert Greenleaf's term, a servant leader. My coauthor and friend Tom Harvey has also been influential. He knew my dad in Pittsburgh and later led Catholic Charities USA and the nonprofit MBA program at the Mendoza School of Management, University of Notre Dame.

The late Fedele Fauri, my first dean, was especially influential as a leadership model as is Lynn Videka, the current Dean of Social Work. Years ago, Marilyn Flynn, presently dean of the University of Southern California Suzanne Dworak-Peck School of Social Work, had the office next to mine; I learned—and continue to learn—from her. Jim Duderstadt, president emeritus of the University of Michigan, and the late Robert Winfield, chief health officer at the University of Michigan, showed exemplary models of leadership and have taught me a great deal. Many of my professors—especially Armand Lauffer, the late Henry J. Meyer, Rosemary Sarri, and the late Robert D. Vinter—were fantastic mentors. Colleagues at the School of Social Work and Ross School of Business, including Bill Birdsall, Jim Blackburn, Jeff DeGraff, Bob Quinn, and Lynn Wooten, are important thought leaders.

Professors and leaders also learn from their students and organizations. Many thanks to my doctoral students and MSW students, whose experiences and insights over the years have been deeply formative. Thanks as well to Warde Manuel, who became athletic director of the University of Michigan in 2016, but who also earned an MSW, MBA, and BA from the university; and thanks to Katherine Gold, MSW MD, Michael Sherraden, and Bowen McBeath. Special thanks goes to my "thinking editor" Beth Zambone, who asks powerful questions, tracks down obscure references, organizes my manuscripts, and skillfully addresses my numerous writing flaws. And special thanks to Dan Madaj for his exceptional help on this manuscript and help and friendship over the years.

A special thanks to my "thinking editor" Beth Zambone, who asks *powerful* questions, tracks down obscure references, organizes my manuscripts, and skillfully addresses my numerous writing flaws.

THE METRICS OF HIGH-PERFORMING ORGANIZATIONS

Organizations need to perform at a high level, and they need to be as good as they can be. What evidence will help us evaluate whether an organization is high-performing, or not? Peter Vaill and others have some suggestions. Vaill (1982) suggests the following categories:

- *Benchmark*

  They are performing well against known external standards.

- *Potential*

  They are performing well against what is assumed to be their potential level of performance.

- *Improvement*

  They are performing well against where they were at some previous point in time.

- *Peer judgement*

  They have been judged by informed observers to be doing substantially better than other comparable systems.

- *Efficiency*

  They are doing what they do with significantly fewer resources than it is assumed they need to do what they do.

- *Exemplars*

  They are perceived as exemplars of the way they do whatever they do and thus become a source of inspiration to others.

- *High culture*

  They are perceived to fulfill, at a high level, the ideals for the culture within which they exist.

- *The only ones*

  They are the only organization that has been able to do what they do at all, even though it might not seem that what they do is a difficult or mysterious thing. To Vaill's suggestions I would add:

- *Value added*

  They provide value in products, services, and system.

- *Nonexploitative*

  They accomplish these tasks without exploiting workers or the environment. Additionally, Jim Collins (2001, 2005) suggests that they:

  - Receive appreciative input
  - Receive awards for high quality
  - Stimulate imitation
  - Are the go-to people

Finally, Leslie Crutchfield and Heather McLeod-Grant (2008) observe that they:

- *Share leadership*

  Encourage leadership from everyone

- *Inspire evangelists*

  Recruit and release those most committed to your mission

- *Nurture nonprofit networks*

  Serve and advocate; work with others

- *Make markets work*

  Partner with commercial organizations who already can reach many of your populations

- *Master the art of adaptation*

  Keep innovating and inventing

What enables high-performing organizations to achieve these lofty benchmarks? Regardless of sector, industry, or size, organizations are composed of people. Quite simply, high-performing organizations engage motivated staff who have the requisite resources and skills to achieve the organization's aim. Effective leaders organize, catalyze, and synthesize this human potential into efficient, effective products and services. Simple enough so far.

However—across sector, industry, and size—the organizational leadership and management picture does not look promising. In recent years we have seen more than the gradual erosion of high expectations. We have witnessed organizations collapse because of faulty leadership and management. We have seen trillions of dollars evaporate as a result of greed and collusion. (See the interesting film *The Big Short* [McKay, 2015].) We have seen humanitarian aid delivered by bureaucratic tortoises and—as a result—children drowning in the Mediterranean surf. To paraphrase, aid denied is like justice denied. When slowed, it causes implementation failure. There are also political conflicts among and between countries and regimes as a result. We have seen thousands of iatrogenic illnesses lead to untimely deaths. This sampling of catastrophic managerial and leadership problems and their tragic consequences does not even begin to account for the millions of unnecessary workaday calls and emails required to prompt promised organizational action in a time characterized by risk aversion, absence of leadership, and half-hearted management. The problem is so familiar that *The New York Times* even features a Sunday column, "The Haggler," which focuses on getting companies to do what they should have done in the first place.

Surely human persons—and the organizations they comprise—have the capacity to work, lead, and manage for the benefit of individuals, communities, and societies. Why, then, are we encountering this tide of bad action, or inaction that produces bad action? There is of course greed and lust for power. But I don't believe most managers and leaders get up in the morning with a plan to ruin people's lives for their own gain. I suspect, more generally, that many don't know what it takes to manage or lead well—and if they do know, they haven't fully developed the skill to consistently implement managerial leadership.

Such uncertainty—when dispersed among teams, which absorb and reflect it—is a huge drain on organizational performance. Because of it, leaders and managers and, consequently, their teams and organizations, reproduce the very patterns they abhor and have promised to change. As reported by Sullivan (2016), Philipp Hensler, who studies how financial advisors responded after the 2008 financial crisis, "asked financial advisors around the United States how they had changed their advisory practices in the wake of the financial crisis. All reported that the financial crash had been a game changer, but 80% responded that they were not doing anything differently" (for specifics of Hensler's research, see Hensler, 2011, 2012).

Rather than a laundry list of practices (as helpful as those are) or a deep dive into one narrow facet of management and leadership practice (as thought-provoking as those are), this book synthesizes my own and others' research and provides readers a *framework* for understanding what good managerial and leadership practice is, evaluating why and how good practices differ from subpar practices, and identifying and developing the tools needed to implement them consistently. In short, it recovers, consolidates, and conveys perennial leadership and management insight in a way that is both intelligible to and useful for 21st-century readers.

To achieve this aim, the book is divided into six parts, which share foundational concepts, skill-building information, and high-performing leadership and management perspectives. Each chapter identifies central concepts, discusses a framework, offers suggestions for reflective practice, and recommends further reading from both perennial and contemporary writers.

Roles and Positions in Organizations

INTRODUCTION

In Part 1, we examine foundational concepts that help us understand what management and leadership are and how they are applied in organizations. Often used interchangeably, the two terms are distinct but related, and cultivating skill in each area is an indispensable part of professional (and personal) success. A few introductory definitions will help us begin clearly.

A *position* is an explicit appointment within a formal organization. In a community benefit organization, common position titles may include *supervisor, manager,* or *executive.* We explore these positions in depth in chapter 1 and throughout the book. A *role,* however, is an attitude or approach that doesn't require an explicit appointment. For example, a person hired as a project manager for a community benefit organization can take on the role of devil's advocate in one meeting and the role of supporter later in the same meeting. Moreover, roles don't exist only within formal professional or volunteer organizations. It's possible to take a leadership role among your neighbors or within your family, for example.

Both are indispensable in your daily life, in the contribution you make to your community benefit organization, and, by extension, the contribution you make to many lives. Be aware, though, that a problem emerges when you become very good at either a management position or a leadership role and overuse one while the other atrophies. Also keep in mind that your personal qualities and skills do not always reflect your position or assignment within an organization or the character of an organization. These divisions are displayed in the boxes in Table P1.1 and P1.2. Sometimes folks in box 1 (Balanced and capable) serve in organizations that are in box 6 (Poorly Managed, poorly led).

Table P1.1. Managerial and Leadership Balance

Management	Leadership High	Leadership Low
High	Balanced and capable manager and leader	Good manager, poor leader
Low	Good leader, poor manager	Poor manager and leader

The relationship between management position and leadership role is best represented by a double helix, as evidenced in Figure P1.1.

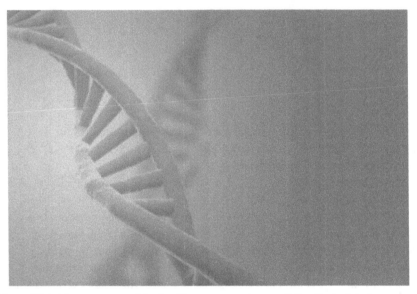

Figure P1.1 Management and leadership competencies are distinct but related.

The helix is also present in the management and leadership structure, as seen in Table P1.2.

Table P1.2. The Management/Leadership Helix

Management	Leadership High	Leadership Low
High	Well managed and led	Well managed, poorly led
Low	Well led, poorly managed	Poorly managed, poorly led

The Competence Staircase

From Novice to Maestro

Whether you start in an entry-level position such as a program coordinator or are hired to fill a more seasoned position such as division manager, you will find yourself on an organizational staircase. Even the flattest, most agile organizations have a staircase—whether implicit or explicit, narrow or broad, steep or gradual.

FOUR STEPS ON THE ORGANIZATIONAL STAIRCASE

Whichever path you take, the appointment to an administrative position is often a first step in a career that leads to positions of greater responsibility and authority. Position names may vary by organization sector, industry, and size, but they fall into three general categories, which I have termed *supervisor, manager (project* and *middle),* and *executive.* Each position has a unique focus, but each involves "accomplishing work through others" although the tools of management and leadership are exercised in different proportions.

Supervisor

As a supervisor, you are in charge of one or more persons. Your purpose is to assist them in accomplishing their jobs in a timely fashion and according to law and policy. You have five primary foci.

> 1. *Professional supervision*
>   Ensuring professionalism.
> 2. *Managerial supervision*
>   Enforcing organizational rules and roles.
>   Supporting optimal organization of work, allocation of time, speed of completion, adherence to due dates, and so on.

3. *Supportive supervision*
   Offering a listening ear.
4. *Developmental supervision*
   Working with the supervisee to develop a career plan and crafting assignments that support that plan.
5. *Reflective supervision*
   Periodically assessing the supervisee's experience and the supervisor/supervisee relationship. Setting general goals for the future.

Supervisors need to be sensitive to these five foci and to be clear with themselves and their supervisees about the area in which they are working at any given moment.

Project Manager

As a project manager, you are responsible for the on-time, on-budget completion of a project in the organization. Project management typically means you are sequencing or linking *jobs, assignments,* and *tasks,* activities that contribute to a larger result, and supervising one or more people assigned to the project. Your supervision focuses on accomplishing the project within temporal, legal, and financial constraints.

Middle Manager

As a middle manager, you are responsible for more than one project or for one much larger project. Middle management involves attention to the organization's mission and is made up of task *bundles*, which are comprised of *jobs* and *assignments*. Middle managers are, like executives, also charged with encouraging and supporting innovation and invention.

Executive Leader

At the C-Level, filling the position of CEO or some other member of the top leadership team, you balance internal organizational oversight with external factors that affect the organization or which the organization wants to affect. You supply meaning and purpose to the organization's employees, clients, consumers, and customers. You are initiating change from strength, not from crises (and not causing too much crisis while encouraging and leading for change).

Table 1.1. Position, Responsibility, Focus, and Activities on the Managerial Staircase

Position	Responsibility	Focus	Activities
Supervisory Manager	Jobs	Assignments	Oversight
Project Manager	Tasks	Projects	Organize
Middle Manager	Work	Systems and Integration	Synchronize and Articulate Parts and Elements
Executive Leader	Purpose and Meaning	Balance Inward and Outward Focus	Initiate and Maintain Change without Crisis

EIGHT FUNCTIONS ON ANY STEP OF THE ORGANIZATIONAL STAIRCASE

After decades of reading management and leadership literature and interviewing hundreds of supervisors, project managers, middle managers, and executives, I have distilled seven essential and perennial functions that characterize successful managers and leaders and high-performing organizations. These functions characterize both individuals in the organization and the organization as a whole, since the well-managed and -led organization fosters a synergy between employees and organization. When that happens, you observe—or experience—1 + 1 = 5, synchrony that is a force multiplier.

1. Performing Efficiently and Effectively

Efficiency means doing things right, following procedures and protocols with as little "drag" as possible, while aiming for optimal performance. Effectiveness means doing the right thing. (Managers can efficiently complete or supervise incorrect or unnecessary tasks.) They have a dual focus on doing the right thing, the right way.

2. Promoting Best Practices (Identifying, Harvesting, Implementing)

Every organization has people who know how to do particular procedures very well. But few organizations identify best practices regularly, and few *harvest*, or gather, these practices for use by the whole organization in any systematic way. When best practices *are* harvested, they may be accompanied by a "people problem": The person who is very good at "X" is viewed as odd or unusual. Hence, the best practice is not accepted because the person who does it best lacks favor.

Successful managers and leaders continually review and refine their own practices, help staff determine what they are especially good at, and record their procedures so that others can use them. They also review these practices for *workout,* taking unnecessary or inappropriate practices and steps out of the system.

3. Employing Data-Driven Decision-Making

Managers and leaders in high-performing community benefit organizations are committed to data-driven decision-making, which relies on qualitative and quantitative evidence rather than organizational lore. Organizational lore develops and persists for a number of reasons, not least because many organizations lack information systems that can easily produce the ongoing quantitative operational data that should comprise at least part of the basis for decision-making. Best practices are best, for example, because they have evidence behind them. Evidence production requires ongoing assessment and evaluation of outcomes and processes. If information systems are inadequate, evaluation becomes a research project, not an ongoing function of the organization.

When evaluation is a "research project," it tends to be a "big deal" and as such stands apart from organizational culture. As such, *evidentiary refurbishment—* new, improved practices within the firm—tend not to enter the picture.

Evaluation works best when you approach it like working out, or gardening. No sensible athlete would say, "I skipped practice all week, so I'll do a 10-hour workout on Saturday." No experienced gardener would ignore his garden all week and spend two 16-hour, back-to-back days catching up. Constant gardening is what is needed, with small, ongoing improvements here and there.

When information systems are adequate and evidence production is a routine organizational function, managers can insert improved practices and procedures and remove old ones with the authority of evidence and the regularity that ensures change is not cataclysmic. As it is, though, organizations are frequently saddled with practices driven by old information, legacy programs that are no longer viable, and founders lobbying to keep things the way they are.

4. Promoting Innovation and Invention

Innovation improves existing procedures and processes. *Invention* adds products and services not yet developed. Improving the menu a restaurant already offers is innovation; adding new dishes is invention. For professional schools, adding new degrees is an invention. For car companies, introducing radically new models (e.g., the Chrysler minivan) is an invention. Invention is related to an organization's core mission, but it is something new in the mission. For example, Zingerman's, a famous Ann Arbor delicatessen, introduced a food rescue business called Food Gatherers—related to food but something it had not done before.

Managers are responsible for encouraging their staff to innovate and improve the job and for overseeing the outcome. They are also charged with fostering invention. Suggestions for innovations and inventions can come from anywhere in the organization or from outside the organization. Middle managers and executive leaders are an important source for innovative and inventive suggestions, not least because they have both an outside and an inside focus. Executives are also responsible for establishing a clear organizational process for piloting innovative and inventive ideas. To free the creativity of employees at all levels of the organizational staircase, though, a clear process must be accompanied by a climate of supportive permission (which has the added effect of preventing the organization from becoming stuck in the mud). In almost all cases, though, innovation and invention require an adjustment in the organization's strategic direction. This has prompted many organizations to create the position of chief strategy officer, a person who assists the top team in thinking through possible innovative and inventive options. The characteristics of an *ideapreneur* are examined in depth in *The Management of Ideas in the Creating Organization* (Tropman, 1998).

5. Developing in This Job and for the Next Job

Successful organizations have a robust program of talent management for all levels of the organization. If there is no organizational budget, however, resourceful managers and leaders (and, less optimally, staff themselves) will direct personal resources toward professional development and write off the expense as an unreimbursed employee expense on their federal return.

6. Providing Talent Management for Workers and Agency

Similarly, however, the organization needs to be supportive of staff development and should be working with each staff member to have a development plan that is at least partially funded by the agency or organization.

Talent management and professional development opportunities are not dispensed at random, though. They are part of a development plan that supports staff in growing in their current positions, becoming better at what they do, and assuming more and different responsibilities. This approach benefits both the organization, which gains enhanced productivity, and the individual, who gains skills in this position, for the next one. Staff need help to develop themselves as professionals in their current job. They need to become better at what they do and soon should begin taking on more and different assignments.

7. Encouraging Staff to Take Leadership Responsibility for Self and Organization

Each step on the organizational staircase—from supervisor to CEO—not only supports the step above but also encourages the level below to take leadership within the organization. Leadership refers not only to exemplary personal conduct but also to overall organizational stewardship. Everyone who works for the organization has a responsibility to take leadership in helping it succeed. A simple example of "taking leadership responsibility" is seen in the harvesting of best practices. When an innovative practice has been developed and refined, it is ready to be presented to the organization, in the local community, or in a broader arena, and managers welcome, facilitate, and help staff prepare for such presentations. Leadership may involve (it usually does involve) some level of risk. Of course, a risk for one may not be a risk for another, but successful managers work through these questions with their staff. As the old phrase has it, "leadership is like manure; it only works when you spread it around."

Leadership can mean many things to many people, and many believe that the specifics of their position are their only responsibilities within the organization. For example, one nonprofit CFO believed her job was, simply, to be the CFO. She was fired because she restricted her insight, interest, and contribution solely to the financial position. When she was asked about the well-being of the organization as a whole, her response was "That is for others [I am not sure which others] to decide." Whether she was working within a suffocating organizational culture or she simply elected to avoid caring about the organization, she was unable—and uncoached—to step up to expand her CFO position to the larger role of organizational leader. One reasonable way to clarify leadership expectations is to add "organizational leadership" and examples to each position description. But regardless of how the organization operationalizes leadership, each of us, whether we work in the corner office or a basement cubicle, can assume a stewarding, caring role that supports organizational success.

8. Securing Appropriate "Visi-Posure" (Visibility + Exposure)

Members of a high-performing organization understand that, in a hyperconnected world, they represent the organization 24/7. They need to behave in ways that bring public credit to the organization and seek out leadership (Rotary, Kiwanis, the Lions) and service (Big Brother/Big Sister, United Way, Red Cross, PTA) opportunities that celebrate their own and the organization's involvement with the health and well-being of the community. Engaging and cultivating a diverse staff that has line-of-sight connections to the organization's products and services also reinforces the organization's commitment to community benefit. Members, especially those in management positions, are careful to avoid narrowly partisan stances at odds with the mission of the organization. This is especially important because such stances not only create incoherence between the organization's image and mission, but they can also affect organizational tax status.

CONCLUSION

In this chapter, we introduced and discussed types of management and leadership, explored the settings in which both are accomplished, and sketched out several perennial characteristics of what management and leadership look like when they are done well. In chapter 2 we build on this foundation to get a detailed sense of the work that managers do, regardless of their position on the organizational staircase.

REFLECTION

- What is the shape of your organization's staircase? Where are you standing? Where do you hope to stand?
- Which of the seven essential functions of management are emphasized in your organization? Which are minimized or overlooked?
- How does this relative prioritization affect (positively or negatively) your organization's performance, your performance, your staff's?

FURTHER READING

Conger, R. (2017). *You go first: Become the leader your team needs.* Eagle, ID: Aloha.
Morgan, J. (2014). *The future of work: Attract new talent, build better leaders, and create a competitive organization.* Hoboken, NJ: Wiley.

2

What Is Managerial Work?

INTRODUCTION

Management, the old adage goes, is the art of accomplishing work through others. What kind of work do managers do to enable others to achieve work? At every level of the organizational staircase, managers manage outputs (activities and events) to outcomes (results).

Increasingly, organizations are structured in teams around jobs, tasks, and other initiatives. What does this look like at various steps on the organizational staircase? The governance team focuses on overall organizational policy, direction, and balance between internal and external priorities. The C-suite team integrates *parts,* products and services, and *elements,* cross-cutting functions that interact with each product or service, across the organization. The middle management/leadership team is responsible for producing products and services and for aligning with element teams to ensure organizational synchrony. Project managers work with a team, budget, and timeline to produce a product, service, or event. (A project could be an ongoing agency function, like client intake or an annual meeting, or it could be a one-time event such as installing a new computer system.) A manager—whether supervisory manager, project manager, middle manager, or senior manager—has several projects or functions under his or her direction that together make up a significant part or element of the organization's product line. What do these distinct teams have in common? Regardless of position or level in the organization, they all are responsible for achieving the organization's mission by facilitating the work of others.

CHANGE AND RESPONSIBILITY AS YOU GO

As you move up the organizational staircase, taking on more and broader management and leadership responsibilities, you keep the tools of the previous stage and add new tools to the mix. It is vital that you retain an appreciation of the previous set of tools, even if you use them differently or less frequently than you did before.

Managers at all levels often—albeit mistakenly—think that their next position is like the former one, only bigger. This misperception leads, perversely, to the increased and more vigorous use of the previous position's tools, rather than the incorporation of new tools appropriate to the new position.

For example, one of the essential elements of supervision is personnel oversight. "Inspect what you expect" is the popular phrase. However, when you move from supervision to project management and leadership, you are suddenly accountable for dates and deliverables; you retain responsibility for personnel supervision, but its execution is handled more by others. If you think that you personally need to engage in more personnel oversight, you risk losing focus on the overall project. Likewise, as a new middle manager, too much checking (micromanaging) or hyper-focus on dates and deliverables means that you are still thinking like a project manager and not doing work of motivating your team or removing future obstacles so that they can perform.

THE NECESSITY OF MANAGEMENT AND LEADERSHIP: GOOGLE THE EVIDENCE

Management and leadership make the world go 'round—albeit often poorly. Many managers really do not know how to manage, and, simply put, they don't do it right.

What is *right?* Google wondered just that, noticing that some managers in its organization achieved excellent results while others . . . didn't. Its People Innovation Lab launched Project Oxygen, a research initiative that used its typical big data/deep dive approach to determine what, if any, specific traits characterized high-achieving managers. Researchers discovered eight characteristics of excellent managers: They are good coaches; they empower and do not micromanage; they care about their staff's personal well-being; they are productive and results oriented; they are good communicators; they support career development; they have a vision; and they use technical skills to advise staff (Garvin, 2013).

Regardless of your current position on the organizational staircase (supervisory, project, middle, or executive), begin with the conviction that your work is vital to the persons, agencies, and communities you serve and the nation, society, and world in which you reside.

Following Project Oxygen, Google realized that the personal skills of individual managers was one part of a high-achieving equation. However, much managerial work is done in teams. And, like managers, some Google teams were more successful than others. So the People Innovation Lab took another deep dive and launched Project Aristotle, which analyzed characteristics of successful and less successful teams.

At the outset, Project Aristotle researchers hypothesized—incorrectly—that the composition of the team would be the deciding factor in its success. As one analyst for Google People Operations reported at the project's conclusion:

Over two years we conducted 200+ interviews with Googlers (our employees) and looked at more than 250 attributes of 180+ active Google teams. We were pretty confident that we'd find the perfect mix of individual traits and skills necessary for a stellar team—take one Rhodes Scholar, two extroverts, one engineer who rocks at AngularJS, and a PhD. Voila. Dream team assembled, right? We were dead wrong. Who is on a team matters less than how the team members interact, structure their work, and view their contributions. So much for that magical algorithm.

We learned that five key dynamics set successful teams apart at Google:

1. *Psychological safety*
   Can we take risks on this team without feeling insecure or embarrassed?
2. *Dependability*
   Can we count on each other to do high quality work on time?
3. *Structure & clarity*
   Are goals, roles, and execution plans on our team clear?
4. *Meaning of work*
   Are we working on something that is personally important for each of us?
5. *Impact of work*
   Do we fundamentally believe that the work we're doing matters?
   (Rozovsky, 2016)

This deep dive into high-performing management and leadership involves harmonizing people and process systems for efficient and effective outcomes. The managers focus on systems as well as persons, even as they work daily with many individual persons. In fact, the persons with whom you work are, mainly, messengers of the systems in which they are functioning, or enmeshed. The legendary manager-scholar Edwards Deming made the point this way: Of all the results we see, 85% of them are due to "common causes of variation" in the system, and 15% are due to individual causes of variation in the person (Deming, 1986). So, the excellent manager, regardless of level, stresses the common causes (systems) and attends to the individual causes (people) (Tropman & Schuester, 2000). Supervisors do this with a person or persons; project managers with several persons and other elements; middle managers with several projects; and executives with strategy, direction, and environment.

THE MANAGER'S META MISSION

Having responsibility for a general system means that managers have some general duties. According to Sayles and Chandler (1971), in their classic *Managing Large Systems*, managers have a general set of responsibilities that encompasses other, more specific duties. To my thinking, these apply, albeit in different proportions at different positions on the organizational staircase, to all managerial and executive work. McCaskey (1982), in *The Executive Challenge: Managing Change and Ambiguity*, has one of the best lists I have seen. According to him, general managerial responsibilities include:

- Taking problems at the right time
- Taking problems in the right order
- Setting and changing decision criteria
- Acting as an organizational metronome

Taking Problems at the Right Time

Managers know at what point a problem needs to be addressed. Appropriate timing depends on many elements, among them project flow (see "Taking Problems in the Right Order") and interpersonal and emotional readiness. For example, when the organization receives bad news, staff tend to react in a pattern, often attributed to Elisabeth Kubler-Ross, referred to as SARAH: shock, anger, rejection, acceptance, and help. Managers who try to address the bad news too early, denying the shock, anger, and rejection (denial) phases, are very unsuccessful. It is better to wait until staff achieve some measure of acceptance; then help is usually welcomed. This is sometimes called "the role of ripeness" (Koestler, 1964).

Taking Problems in the Right Order

All managers have encountered situations that have a "hierarchy of needs." Certain problems must be resolved before others can be addressed. Managers need to ensure that antecedent procedures and processes are ready so that subsequent ones can begin. The Guttmann Scale, PERT chart, and critical path (discussed in detail in chapter 11) are vital in helping managers determine the appropriate timing and order for addressing problems.

Setting and Changing Decision Criteria

Managers set criteria for their own decision-making and that of their area of jurisdiction. When doing so, they need to give general priorities—guidance that bridges the space between policy on the one hand and details of implementation on the other. Such guidance parallels "commander's intent," an approach to military decision-making (Dempsey & Chavous, 2013).

The concept of [an] operation is the most important part of the order and, since the 1990s, most of our Army has not done this well. The result is that we tend to overwrite intent and then go immediately into a detailed scheme of maneuver. It is one of the reasons why we often tend to fall out of plans prematurely. The concept is the only element of an order in which commanders communicate how all of their forces will combine efforts to accomplish the mission. It should cover the type of offensive, defensive, reconnaissance, or security operation; describe forms of maneuver; identify formations; describe actions on contact; describe the timing of the operation; define the cooperation between maneuver forces at critical points in the fight; and describe how all arms will be coordinated. In short, the concept is important because it explains how the commander visualizes the operation—it tells the story of the operation or battle. A good concept permits units to take initiative within the intent and assists subordinate commanders in nesting their efforts with their higher headquarters and adjacent units (McMaster, 2005).

But "commanders" (manager/leaders) in all organizations need to establish decision criteria. If you "command" a McDonald's franchise, for example, then *fast* and *food* are two decision criteria for your staff. But do you intend all staff to prioritize both criteria equally? Perhaps your priority is to maximize purchases, in which case you ask some units to prioritize *fast* and others *food*. Your staff need to know your overarching goal, the criteria you've set for decision-making, and the parameters within which they can alter their "on the ground" strategy as circumstances dictate.

Acting as an Organizational Metronome

Like a metronome or a conductor who sets the tempo for a musician's or an orchestra's performance, managers set the tempo of their organization's performance. They set the level of urgency with which tasks and projects are undertaken, which contributes to the overall organizational pace. As with music performance, organizational pace varies. Some run at a pokey pace: Deliverables are promised in time frames much longer than are needed; requests are processed as if staff are in slow motion, or under water; chattiness trumps work; staff even walk slowly. Others are always in crisis—running from problem to emergency to urgent priority—running staff at an intense pace without taking into account the need for encouraging morale or pacing for endurance. Only a few organizations run at a prompt, unruffled tempo. But here, work is effective and efficient; change happens quickly; there is a culture of haste without waste and focus without distress. Whether an organization's tempo lags behind, races uncontrollably, or moves crisply and unhindered, the pace is set by its leaders.

CONCLUSION

In this chapter, we looked at what it means to be a high-achieving manager (and why it matters), where managers fit in an organization, and what their general system-level duties are. In chapter 3, we move to a specific examination of the tools that enable managers to accomplish these general responsibilities and to "achieve work through others."

REFLECTION

- Do your responsibilities as a manager or leader incorporate the general responsibilities McCaskey outlines?
  Taking problems at the right time
  Taking problems in the right order
  Setting and changing decision criteria
  Acting as an organizational metronome
- For each, identify a specific case in which you succeeded and one in which you could have improved.
- What factors influenced your success (or lack thereof)?

FURTHER READING

Bock, L. (2015). *Work rules! Insights from inside Google that will transform how you live and lead.* London, U.K.: John Murray.

McCaskey, M. (1982). *The executive challenge: Managing change and ambiguity.* New York, NY: HarperCollins.

3

PSOSBPE

The Managerial Toolkit

How are the general managerial duties, discussed in chapter 2, actually achieved? Depending on an organization's size and sector, and the position a manager occupies on the organizational staircase, the tools of community benefit organizational management and leadership are various combinations of the following elements:

- Planning
- Strategizing
- Organizing
- Staffing
- Budgeting
- Programming
- Evaluating

I call this toolkit PSOSBPE. These are the essential tools of the administrative trade, and they are used throughout the managerial career, albeit at increasing levels of generality. You do not always use them in this order, although it is common for a new initiative. For existing operations, simply ensure that the flow of the plan is smooth. It should be laid out in broad strokes, with the goals and the steps in rough sequence. Its strategy should contain key elements of the plan and make a series of decisions about sequence and fit. Organizing requires more specificity about the kinds of activities needed to make the plan come to fruition. Staffing identifies people needed, while budgeting contemplates dollars needed. Programming involves designing and offering the actual product, service, meal, performance, and so on. Evaluation involves constant review and readjustment based on change circumstances. (Budgeting occurs later in the process. This location is no accident. Money always serves goals, not the reverse. Early discussion of finances is usually too big a burden for projects, as realistic figures cannot be ascertained until significant research has been completed.)

PLANNING

In this phase, you and your team set goals for an initiative. "Start with the end in mind," and the general, overall steps that will get you there (Covey, 1990). All planning has this component, whether planning your day, a course of treatment, an evening meal, or a staff retreat. Without planning, nothing works very well. The other phases require the discipline of a plan. However, the plan is a guideline, and it shouldn't be seen as a cement overcoat or as license to throw practicalities out the window. Critics of planning usually overstate how firm the plan is or how impractical it is. From this fallacious perspective, they assert that planning is foolish, whether because the context is so dynamic or the resources so limited.

High-performing manager/leaders invite their staff to draft plans for goal achievement and use them to begin goal-setting discussions; Exceptions to this guideline come when the law or the agency sets requirements (e.g., in government or other contracts). In this case, the statute or the Request For Proposal (RFP) has already done the planning. Planning addresses, but does not always answer, general questions like:

- What is our broad aim?
- What outcomes do we want to achieve?
- What are the general procedures by which we might achieve these ends?

STRATEGIZING

When strategizing, you and your team lay out potential courses of action (e.g., best case, worst case, exit) using the goals you identified in the planning phase. Strategizing should aim for a *strategic plan*—a focused but flexible overall approach to the initiative, game, or career. What will you do if events unfold in one direction? in another? Do you have a plan for capitalizing on unexpected success or minimizing unforeseen difficulties? The wise manager and team lay these options out in advance of launching the initiative since, as people say, the person with some plans in his or her pocket is usually better off than the one who doesn't. But these should be guidelines rather than straightjackets.

Courses of action have risks and rewards, and in the strategy phase both need to be considered. There is no risk-free option. Not all options are high risk, though. The level of risk an initiative can bear depends on a number of factors—not least the goals identified in the plan, the risk tolerance of the team or organization, the external environment, and the potential for reward. Consider the financial sector: Investing in bonds provides some security but exposes one to inflationary risk. Equity investments help capture growth gain but expose investors to market turbulence. Retaining traditional products is comfortable but fails the innovation/invention test. New programs, on the other hand, may not perform as expected.

Whether positioning self or organization, strategy requires constant decision-making. And there is no "non-decision" position. ("Not to decide is to decide.") Executive leaders are constantly involved in the process of strategic decision-making in pursuit of *strategic advantage*: succeeding with one product or service and using it to position the next product or service for success. Strategic decision-making in pursuit of strategic advantage has much in common with the game of eight ball. Player 1 has a cue ball in the center of the table and the opportunity for a sure shot at player 2's ball resting in front of the side pocket: a conservative, safe approach. Alternatively, player 1 has a shot at player 2's ball in a corner pocket, with a high probability of success *and* the added advantage of positioning the cue for one, possibly two, subsequent shots. The second opportunity confers *strategic advantage*.

Team strategizing discussions contemplate questions such as:

- What are the risks and decisions involved?
- Do we have a strategic plan?
- If not, what course of action will help us achieve our goals?
- Do we have Plan B (C, D, and E)?
- What resources do we need, and when?
- How will we monitor and measure progress?
- What might get in the way? How could we respond and adapt?
- How does this strategic plan align with our goals? Is any part incoherent?

ORGANIZING

Organizing, sometimes called operational planning, bridges the gap between your goal and its achievement. As such, it takes a much more practical, detailed, near-term approach than a strategic plan. While a strategic plan focuses on a general course of action in pursuit of a goal, an operational plan focuses on practical implementation and lays out, in weekly and daily detail, how you'll accomplish it. Operational plans are often characterized by a specific timeframe and have specific and measurable intermediate goals. They tend to be team-specific, rather than organization-wide, and also—when well-conceived—support the operations of other teams within the organization. Reporting occurs at regular, frequent intervals and responds to progress toward specific milestones. This provides ample opportunity for course correction during the life of the plan. Typically, operational planning conversations with your team focus on questions like:

- Where are we now?
- Where do we want to be?
- How do we get there?
- How do we measure progress?

Two of its key components are staffing and budgeting.

STAFFING

Staffing identifies people needed to accomplish a task, answering the question *who*: Who will we need for this project, and when? What kind of team needs to be assembled? What is the skill mix we will need? Sometimes an initiative involves many people, both permanent and as needed. At other times it seems a team is comprised of "just" or "only" a single person. Even in such situations, a number of relationships are involved: manager and staff member, colleagues and vendors, and informal personal contacts. Staffing involves several elements:

- Recruiting (internally or externally)
- Onboarding
- Training
- Supervising
- Directing
- Training
- Educating
- Coaching
- Evaluating
- Ongoing motivating

BUDGETING

Budgeting allocates resources over the life of the initiative. In this phase, you apportion finite resources and practically prioritize how you will fund (with both money and time) the operational plan. Money we understand, but less explicit is the reality that *time* involves "hidden inventory," or the time that people, including you, need to invest to staff the initiative.

Budgeting is, in several senses, a control function. When you budget, you look to the future, focusing on both the input of temporal and financial resources and the output that results. A budget is a transition matrix, if you will, morphing anticipated inputs (funding) into anticipated outputs (allocations).

Of course, uncertainties emerge throughout these processes. For example, an initiative's funding may not materialize, or it may exceed expectations. Actual expenses differ from anticipated expenses, and time can be gobbled up by this, that, and the other thing. But the need to prestructure these allocations (even in a general way) is crucial to management and leadership at all levels. Budgets not only provide controls; they also provide goals or targets toward which investments should be made. For example, an organization's goal may be to hold its annual meeting for $10,000. This goal can also be a control: The organization only has $10,000 available for this event.

We spend significant time talking about financial budgets, but we must also budget our time. Time management and leadership (see chapter 5) is nothing more or less than a time budget. Like a financial budget, it controls the amount of time you spend on any one aspect of the initiative. It, too, is a control: You must not exceed the budgeted amount. Time budgets are crucial in initiatives without natural temporal boundaries. For example, I teach a class that meets for one hour three times each week. I have to fit my material into the available time, as others will use the room after me, and my students have other commitments. But much community benefit work lacks such boundaries.

Meetings, which we examine in detail later (see chapter 13), are a prime example. Time and meetings are a real problem, both in terms of the time spent on any item within a meeting and the total number of hours spent in these meetings. Managers need to run excellent meetings, regardless of purpose, size, or stakes. A time budget is a great place to start improving your meeting leadership. And while time budgeting in meetings and for meetings will be a huge help, the decision-making process of budgeting is broadly applicable.

PROGRAMMING/IMPLEMENTING

Programming is launching and running the product, event, or service—offering the new menu, launching the new product. Preparation, launch, and implementation look different depending on an organization's size, the sector in which it serves, and the purpose of the initiative. It is possible, though, to identify some common elements. These include but are not limited to whether the initiative requires an individual or team approach, the level of permissions required, and so on. Generally the bigger and older the organization is, the slower the "art-to-part" or "bench-to-bedside" process is. (This is why some organizations prefer to develop new services or products outside the organization and bring them in.) The initial step in this process is the idea. Usually it arrives in a package like, "What about?" or "Suppose we," "Could we try . . . ?" or "Let's pilot." Once the idea has the green light, then, usually, a proposal is developed outlining steps and costs. The third step is a prototype of the idea. Once the prototype has been developed, one moves to testing—usually alpha and then beta testing.

Alpha and beta testing are useful preparation for launch. While the distinction between the two can be less than crisp, alpha testing focuses on intramural, or in-house, review, and beta testing targets customers and other end users. Most products include both alpha *and* beta test phases; both are valuable for discovering bugs or glitches. Some organizations use terms such as field trials, prerelease, customer validation, customer acceptance testing, user acceptance testing, and beta testing synonymously. Moreover, both phases often shift their goals and methods in real-time based on ongoing results.

EVALUATING

Evaluation is multifaceted. Here I touch on evaluating people, product, and process. When evaluating people, you focus on employees, interns, direct reports, and so on. When evaluating product, you focus on the deliverables—outcomes, of course, but also outputs and, in many instances, products. In the community benefit organization, it is sometimes easy to conflate people and product since, often (in counseling, for example), the people deliver the product. We'll begin with people, then look at product or outcome, and then consider the combination of the two.

People

It turns out that Socrates' dictum, "the unexamined life is not worth living," applies in modified form to supervision as well. Management and leadership require constant goal setting, monitoring, overseeing, assessing, feeding back, and improving information that emerges from evaluation. In short, evaluation helps the organization benefit from living an examined life.

No evaluation is possible if goals are not established during the planning and strategizing phases and tracked during subsequent phases. Typically, these goals are mutually agreed upon between the supervisee and the manager/leader. Following that, monitoring—whether formal or informal—involves benchmarks that need to be accomplished by the supervisee and/or the supervisor so the process can move forward. These can be relatively automatic. Oversight (inspect what you expect) consists of periodic check-in meetings during which the supervisor and the supervisee can assess the extent to which everyone is on target. If oversight is quarterly, then assessment is a midcourse meeting during which the overall progress is judged. There is a third-quarter oversight meeting and then a final "performance appraisal" during which goal achievement is checked and a "grade" given.

Evaluation has two front-end components that run through this process: feedback and grading. *Feedback* consists of simple tips on how the supervisee's performance might be improved. *Grading* reflects a qualitative, though evidence-based, judgment on how well the supervisee did. The front end of the evaluation process is heavily feedback centered; as time moves along, grading becomes more important, and, in the appraisal meeting, grading is the most powerful component. Grading involves judgment of whether the supervisee is working to or above standard. It occurs in a relationship in which the grader is more powerful than the "gradee."

Of all tasks, managers seem to hate performance appraisal the most, and they do it poorly and irregularly, if at all. This task avoidance sparks a negative self-fulfilling prophecy: Little experience results in task avoidance, which in turn produces limited experience and more avoidance, and so on. It is no wonder performance appraisal is heartily disliked in organizations.

Yet some people excel at performance appraisal. Music teachers, cooking instructors, and coaches are but a few examples of professions where evaluation is a constant, ongoing process. It can be done well, and for high-quality work must be done well. We will discuss more about feedback communication in chapter 8, "Managing Subordinates."

The final step is that the evaluator, working with program administration and staff, needs to translate the results of the evaluation research into actual changes in program practices. Typically, thoughts about the translation process are thought about during the initial goal setting phase and in the organization of the programming, but that is not always the case.

Managers also need assessment of their performance. The 360° approach often works well. In this method, the manager secures feedback from subordinates, superiors, peers, the external network, and his or her self (and family). Results are usually given to an outside evaluator who digests and synthesizes them and presents feedback on patterns to the manager/leader.

Product

Product evaluation begins with a distinction between outputs, or activity, and outcomes, or results: The patient gets better; substance abuse is controlled; weight is lost; smoking habits change; the neighborhood is measurably safer. The key here is *measurably*. To manage products, you need metrics that are *reliable*, or able to yield consistent results, and *valid*, or accurately measure the specific concept under consideration. There are additional criteria, however. Most prominent are time and budget. Outcomes must be accomplished within a certain amount of time and within cost parameters. The overall goal, even in a community benefit organization, is "faster, better, cheaper" via ethical means.

Process

Organizations are made up of work processes, often called *systems*. Depending on organization context, size, and complexity, it will have systems for human processes (compensation, sharing information, hiring and firing, and so on) and production processes (steps to achieve outputs and outcomes). Organizations should regularly review all systems for functionality, effectiveness, and efficiency—determining whether they do the right things and whether they do things right. Organizations do not typically evaluate processes until something difficult transpires. Sometimes (as in a meeting when a difficult item or decision is to be discussed later and never is), there is never any review. In the case of meetings, my research suggests that most organizations meet twice as often or as long as needed, at a cost of hundreds of billions of dollars.

APPROACHES TO MANAGEMENT

There are lots of ways in which managers can improve the work they do, regardless of their position on the organizational staircase. I mention several here, and—if they are discussed in detail elsewhere in the book—reference the chapter where I examine them.

Manage by Wandering Around

In chapters 10 to 12, we examine in detail how managers can connect with various aspects of the initiative and stay "in the loop" with receiving input and offering feedback. (Remember, managers harmonize systems, which often includes cultivating relationships within and outside the organization. See chapter 2.)

Developed by Tom Peters, "managing by wandering around" (MBWA) encourages managers to get out of their office and touch base with workers and others informally (Peters & Waterman, 1982). It is useful for monitoring and oversight, and it also gets you out of your office and away from the trappings of power that your office conveys. There are some important elements to remember when practicing MBWA. One is to not react to what you see and hear at that time. Store it away and, if necessary, talk with staff later in private. Staff cubicles are not a good place to do serious business.

Practice the Eight-Ball Principle

This principle addresses achieving goals while simultaneously increasing the probability of achieving other goals. When thinking with the eight-ball principle, you focus on both here-and-now *and* there-and-then issues. You might choose to do something now because it has the potential to place you in a strategic position later. Pool players and chess aficionados will recognize this principle immediately: A good shot is sinking your target. A better shot is sinking your target and positioning your cue ball for the next shot. The best shot is selecting your target on the basis of positioning, which positions you for the immediate next shot and the next several shots as well.

Walk the Talk: Act With Integrity

Everyone has heard this cliché. But clichés are repeated often enough to become a cliché because they convey a certain element of truth. Walking the talk, or living with integrity, means, simply, that you do what you say you are going to do. That is a definition of integrity in anyone's book. Because example is such a powerful teacher, it is essential that you follow through on your commitments if you want others to do the same. (And it is the right—the ethical and professional and leadership—thing to do.)

Employ the Pinball Principle

Kidder (1981) suggested the pinball principle as an explanation of why engineers worked day and night to build a new computer with little additional financial reward: If they succeeded, their success entitled them to more notice and more projects of interest. His general formulation, applicable to all managers, is that praise and support for employees goes a long way. Use it.

Use the Two Ears/One Mouth Ratio

We have two ears and one mouth. That ratio is a useful guide to the appropriate proportion of listening to talking behavior. Generally, managers should listen twice as much as they talk. Talking is one of those cases where, often, "less is more." If you're a talker, or you don't know how to encourage non-talkers to be talkers, encourage with open-ended questions, and practice being okay with not saying everything you know, with pauses or breaks in a conversation.

Uncertainty Absorption; Authoritative Augmentation

As managers, you have more power than those below you on the organizational staircase. This power differential creates two kinds of experience for managers and leaders, regardless of where they are on the organizational staircase. The first is uncertainty absorption. As March and Simon (1958) explain, *uncertainty absorption* is the "inference structure" of an organization. It occurs when "inferences are drawn from a body of evidence and the inferences, instead of the evidence itself, are communicated" (p.165). Uncertainty absorption is heightened, I would add, when inferences are communicated as fact, with particular emphasis on removing or narrowing the variance generated by the uncertainty (see Table 3.1).

Table 3.1. Uncertainty Absorption/Authority Augmentation

Worker to Executive			Executive to Worker		
Worker	Manager	Executive	Executive	Manager	Worker
Good News	Good News	Good News	Suggestion	Order	Requirement
Bad News	Bad News	Bad News	Question	Order	Requirement
Uncertain News	Uncertain News	Uncertain News	Opinion	Truth	Policy

As a manager, knowing the uncertainty principle allows you to be more cautious when examining the accuracy of information reported from staff. When communicating up, staff tend to use a preferred sequence of information:

- Good news
- Bad news
- Uncertain news

The last is least desirable because the messenger feels he or she looks worst when delivering it. Thus, as staff "report up" they tend to convert the uncertain into the more certain, and probabilities (with lots of variance) become certainties (either good or bad). The information you get is almost always more "firm" than is actually the case.

When you augment your authority, *you* add certainty to the organization, but you are conveying it "downward." When a manager asks a question or thinks out loud, the message becomes more authoritative and certain as it moves down the organizational staircase. Thus "I wonder if . . . ?" or "Could it be that . . . ?" or "Would you look into . . . ?" becomes "Jim insists that . . . !" and "Lloyd says do it!" and "We never . . . because James can't stand it." Like a snowball picks up speed going downhill, tentativeness at the top becomes imperative and certain as it rolls down the organization. As one example, a Ford executive driving into work reportedly looked out the window and observed a parking lot full of Ford cars. Out of curiosity, he asked his secretary, "Why do we have hundreds of cars parked in the lot by the freeway?" When he drove home that afternoon, the lot was empty. His curiosity had been interpreted as a command.

CONCLUSION

Management and leadership is the art of getting work done through others. While chapter 2 explored managerial duties generally, this chapter introduced the foundational tools, PSOSBSE, that managers and leaders in any position on the organizational staircase use to achieve work through others. Now that we've considered managerial work and how high-achieving managers do it, let's examine the context in which they work, the organization.

REFLECTION

- Think about managers whose work you admire: What management style(s) do they tend to employ? When and why do they shift styles? Where do they tend to be weakest/strongest? Identify a specific example of each.

- Now turn the camera on to your own managerial approach. What are your default management styles? When, why, and how do you shift modes? What are your weakest/strongest approaches?
- Which aspects of your PSOSBSE toolkit would you like to strengthen? What specifically would you like to be able to do as a result of investing in these aspects?

FURTHER READING

Bossidy, L., & Charan, R. (2014). *Execution: The discipline of getting things done.* New York, NY: Crown Business.

Meyers, G. C. (1986). *When it hits the fan: Managing the nine crises of business.* New York, NY: Houghton Mifflin Harcourt.

Understanding Organizations

Organizations have both cultural and structural features that shape how one leads and manages at all levels on the organizational staircase. In part 2, we shift our focus from the work that managers and leaders do in organizations to the structure of organizations themselves. We develop a framework for understanding organizations and the activity that is characteristic of them.

4

What Is an Organization?

Management happens everywhere. You'll find that you manage yourself, manage at home, at school, and in the neighborhood. We may not think so, but we are always managing—or not managing. Our focus in this volume is on the management and leadership that take place in formal organizations. (As you probably know, management and leadership in organizations are often useful in the family and community. But be alert: Treating your family as staff leads to trouble; treating employees as family is similarly problematic. Customize your crossovers, and manage yourself first.) But to adequately understand and transform management in this context, we need to have a clear grasp of what an organization actually is and how an organization's structure influences the management and leadership that unfold within it.

WHY DOES IT MATTER?

Organizational structure matters because it is largely the organization and its structure, rather than individuals within it, that produce (or don't produce) the results we hope to achieve. As mentioned in chapter 2, Edwards Deming (1982) argues that 85% of what the organization produces is organization-driven, and only 15% can be attributed to individual action. Deming calls these "common causes of variation" and "unique causes of variation." The reason it is so important for us to talk about the organization lies in this insight. American society tends to think about the relationship between organizations and individuals in a way diametrically opposed to Deming's insight: It prioritizes and privileges the individual rather than attending to the organizational (and social) structure. In short, we focus on "Harry" when we should focus on "Harry's department."

To effectively and efficiently manage and lead within formal organizations, it is therefore important to understand their structure. Management and leadership may, indeed, be "accomplishing work through others," but it is the structure within which work happens, as well as the connections among others, and the sequences of those connections, that distinguish between mediocre and high-performing organizations. In fact, a better phrase to describe management might be "getting work done *with* others."

A TASTE OF ORGANIZATIONAL THEORY

Organizations are one of the ways in which society organizes itself, and formal organizations have some common features. The foci of varied social science disciplines help us to develop a nuanced understanding of what an organization is. The descriptions here are brief and oversimplified, but if you keep them in mind during our discussion—and as you grow in the organization—you'll have a better grasp on the context in which you manage and lead.

Anthropology: Considers the culture of organizations, their ideas, values, norms, and beliefs. It tends to see organizations as "patterns of culture" (Benedict, 1934). Feelings and commitments are important as are values and norms. But anthropologists see practices and artifacts as a part of culture as well.

Economics: Views organizations as if they were composed of rational individuals maximizing their own fortunes. A winner-takes-all perspective prevails here.

Political science: Political scientists see organizations as fields of power. From a political science perspective, organizational members see power as organizational currency and seek to maximize the power they have.

Psychology: Tends to view the organization from an interior perspective and sees organizations as packages of individual characteristics. It examines the temperament, their "emotion quotient," and the communication style of individuals who comprise organizations.

Sociology: The product of the organization is delivered by the system itself, and individual employees are the messengers. Like anthropologists, sociologists see systems and connections between systems and subsystems as key to understanding organizations.

Now that we have a (very brief) overview of how the social sciences conceptualize organizations, let's zoom in and unpack the components of this collection of systems and individuals we call an organization.

ORGANIZATIONAL THEORIES

Various thinkers have tried to define or describe organizations. Max Weber (1946) is perhaps the most famous. He suggests that organizations have the following elements:

- Division of labor (The Organization)
- Administrative apparatus
- Hierarchy of authority
- Impersonal rules
- Full-time jobs/careers

These elements—while most of us can relate to them—describe more professional, mature, or developed organizational forms. Organizations at the beginning of the organizational growth cycle (entrepreneurial or startup organizations) may have a minimal division of labor, elementary administrative apparatus, murky authority structure and personnel rules, and unclear jobs with uncertain career potential. Indeed, one challenge organizations face is forming this unorganized beginning into a more formal structure. Managers and leaders have the challenge of adapting their working style to both the entrepreneurial and the professional organization.

The organizational analyst Robert Quinn (1988) studied organizations in terms of core elements: clan, bureaucracy, market, and adhocracy. According to Quinn, clan organizations are characterized by loyalty and commitment, like fraternities. Bureaucratic organizations are characterized by rules and rituals. (These most closely resemble Weber's model.) Market organizations are defined only by results. "What have you done for me today?" is the hallmark question. Adhocracy (from the Latin *ad hoc*, or "to this") organizations are driven by ideas and by doing the new, single thing. From Quinn's perspective, managers and leaders have the challenge of communicating to an organization's dominant culture, while simultaneously effecting a balance between the dominant culture and other subcultures in the organization, as well as among those subcultures.

Bohlman and Deal (2003) suggest *prisms* or *frames* as ways to understand organizations. They identify three primary frames: human resource (people), political (power, conflict), and symbolic (cultural). Each frame yields a different insight about the organization. Managers and leaders have the challenge of considering each: people, power, and culture.

ELEMENTS AND FOCI OF ORGANIZATIONS

Organizations have formal and informal elements. The formal elements are reflected in the organizational chart, which encapsulates one aspect of the organization. Organizations also have informal elements, reflected in connections that cross formal organizational lines and through which communication flows. They also convey who likes whom, who is the "go to" person on what subjects, who will go the extra mile to finish a project, and so on. The informal system is the repository of personal information about people in the organization, the place where judgments about each person's quality and character are made and kept, and the locus of organizational gossip. Managers and leaders in high-performing organizations are aware of both elements and how to appropriately use either, depending on the situation.

Organizations have both task and process foci. A *task focus* stresses organizational goals (outputs and outcomes), accomplishments, and achievements. A *process focus* stresses the emotional and social climate of the organization and attends to items like compassion at work. Often staff specialize in contributing to one focus or the other. Frequently, the leadership of a process contributor (who organizes birthday parties, announces deaths, provides office decorations, and coordinates meals for employees who are ill) is underappreciated. While both task and process foci are needed, the latter is often what makes an organization a great place to work. Excellent managers celebrate and reward those who contribute organizational tasks as well as those who give attention to process.

Understanding these elements and foci (and others) is helpful in achieving managerial and organizational goals, but managers and leaders must recognize that organizations, as entities, have a reality of their own. Managers and leaders work within an organizational context that has certain—sometimes unhealthy—forces acting upon it.

THE DARK SIDE OF ORGANIZATIONS

Organizations often develop problems in their functioning, some of which become part of their character. We usually see the darker side of organizational behavior when it becomes public (e.g., the pedophilia scandal and subsequent cover-up that have plagued the Roman Catholic church; Enron's debt concealment to improve the bottom line; the compounded events that comprise the #metoo movement or those that influence the #blacklivesmatter movement). These public displays of organizational corruption do not emerge from a vacuum. They usually incubate in one or more "dark" organizational traits that result in very public consequences. For example, de Vries and Miller (1984) look at the "crazy making" organization in which the culture itself is "sick" and needs to be fundamentally changed. We discuss just a few next.

Oligarchy

Organizations small and large tend to be run by a small group. This tendency generates a tension between openness and involvement of staff on one hand, and my-way-or-the-highway on the other. *Authority*, formal, legitimate power authorized by a governance process, is generally a good thing. It is distinct from *authoritative*, which is informal legitimate power deriving from knowledge and expertise. However, it can easily become *authoritarian*, the overuse, and capricious use, of either formal or informal power. Unlike authority, this is usually not good.

Conflation of Means and Ends

Organizations develop means (outputs) to achieve ends (outcomes). It is fairly common for some displacement to occur: Means replace ends, means continue when ends have changed, or any means are used to justify ends.

An organization requires policy systems *and* practice systems to accomplish its mission. When the distance between these two systems becomes too great, the organization displays multiple personalities and employees get two sets of directives—one formally, via channels outlined in the organizational chart, and the other informally, via gossip or a general "sense" in the organizational atmosphere. Here, the organization is characterized by unhealthy patterns and an atmosphere of low trust and low morale. De Vries and Miller (1984) call this organization neurotic. This can also be a form of *means ritualism,* a phrase coined by Merton (1957) in *Social Structure and Process* to describe what occurs when procedures developed to achieve earlier ends change and continue, though they are no longer relevant.

Defensive Routines

The "pathology" of organizations is not only something that drives employees crazy; it also causes a lot of harmful behavior to the social system in which it lives. The film *The Corporation* deals with such abuse. A *New York Times* review observes:

> The film . . . half-mockingly offers a psychiatric diagnosis based on a list of abuses that arise from the relentless pursuit of profit. The point is not that individual companies pollute the environment, hurt animals, exploit workers, and commit accounting fraud, but that such outrages are a result of the essential personality traits of the corporate life form. These behaviors are symptoms arising from a list of pathologies that includes "disregard for the well-being of others," "inability to form lasting relationships," and "deceitfulness." A psychiatrist who has advised the FBI declares the corporation has "all the characteristics of a prototypical psychopath." (Scott, 2004)

All natural and social systems require good information if they are to survive and flourish. Predators need to know where prey live and how to catch them; prey need to know the patterns of predators and how to avoid them. The survival of each depends upon good (but not complete) information. Organizations and agencies also need information, and they need to discuss and act on it. In particular the organization needs to address "bad news" in whatever form it takes: financial, human resources, customer/consumer dissatisfaction, and so on. Organizations, like the individuals who comprise them, often tend to deny bad news and not discuss it, because they fear the consequences that might emerge from that discussion.

Argyris (1985) points out that the oligarchy that controls organizations and agencies often engages in practices in which manager and leaders *fail to discuss* key items and instead engage in "defensive routines." Essentially, defensive routines mean that some things in organizations (and, by extension, families) are not discussed. Additionally, their nondiscussability is not discussed. One organizational wag calls this kind of behavior "rearranging deck chairs on the Titanic." Usually the organization or family flounders along until public disaster strikes (e.g., the CEO flees with his assistant and the endowment).

Defensive routines support failure to act on information. They resemble boiled frog syndrome (discussed in chapter 14), which alleges that if you place a frog in a pan of cold water and slowly raise the temperature of that water over a Bunsen burner, the frog will not notice that the water is getting hotter, will remain in the pan, and will boil to death. Alternatively, if you place a frog in a pan of hot water it will jump right out. In organizational analysis, the frog's problem is called the "just noticeable difference syndrome." Some organizations never act on information that has not changed significantly since the last time they looked at it. Hence, slowly evolving trends are missed. Environments around organizations are always changing. If they change quickly the organization will usually try to respond. If they change slowly, it may be more dangerous because today does not look that different from yesterday. Managers delay action until something hits the fan: Avoidance of problems is generally not a good strategy.

PSYCHIC INCOME AND IMPAIRED DIGNITY AT WORK

What happens at work deeply forms our sense of meaning, or *psychic income* (Tropman, 2001) and *dignity at work*, being treated well at and by work (Hodson, 2001). According to Hodson, a number of circumstances can impair or destroy dignity at work. They include:

- Mismanagement and abuse
- Overwork
- Autonomy constraint
- Denial and rejection of employee involvement

Mismanagement and Abuse

Abusive managers are either interpersonally (physically or emotionally) abusive or are responsible for permitting an abusive environment by failing to provide a coherent workplace. Coherence—or the failure to provide the supplies and equipment needed to do the required job while simultaneously expecting staff to work faster and do more—is a form of social exploitation. Carey (2004) writes: "Enduring an abusive boss is one of the more common problems I work with as an organizational consultant. (One CEO brought a squirt gun to his staff meetings!)" Solomon (1990/2002) suggests several types of problematic bosses, and I offer a few suggestions for working with them.

1. Hostile, angry, belligerent
   Ask "Is there anything else?" Try not to let their anger create anger in you.
2. Pushy, presumptuous, arrogant
   Set narrow limits; remind them that others have needs as well.

3. Deceitful, deceptive, underhanded
   Ask for material in writing; These folks are often verbally skillful; you need a chance to review in advance and prepare. Seek legal backup.
4. Shrewd, manipulative, exploitative
   Provide limits in advance within which this person needs to work.
5. Discourteous, rude, abrasive
   Remind this person that courtesy is always appropriate.
6. Egotistical, self-centered, self-seeking
   Assign this person tasks that involve helping others.
7. Procrastinating, vacillating, delaying
   Set specific limits with consequences.
8. Rigid, obstinate, unbending
   Provide alternatives from which they can choose.
9. Tight-lipped, taciturn, uncommunicative
   Invite them to share; assign them jobs which require oral participation.
10. Complaining, critical, fault-finding
    Ask them to be the "Angel's advocate" (taking the positive side of a point for a change).

Overwork

Overwork *exploits* staff, requiring them to work cheap or free, and (or) it *conscripts* them, extracting work while denying them choice or compensation. We find overwork in "forced overtime," involuntary shift changes, and the expectation of "commitment." We've all heard the approving statement, "Sally will always go the extra mile." Of course, it's good to go the extra mile—occasionally. But it's not appropriate for managers and leaders to expect extra-mile performance consistently without compensation, though such expectations often emerge in community benefit organizations.

Autonomy Constraint

Also known as micromanagement and over-checking, autonomy constraint tends to produce the errors anxious or inexperienced managers hope they will prevent. They also convey to staff an insecurity-producing lack of trust, since all workers, but especially professional workers, need some say in how they carry out their responsibilities. Once goals are given, staff should enjoy *means freedom,* a sense that they can approach the responsibility in a way that they choose (within appropriate organizational and legal limits, of course). When that autonomy is constrained through micromanaging, staff are devalued and undignified.

Denial of Employee Involvement

Hodson's fourth category of dignity impairment involves keeping employees in the dark about organizational strategy, surprising them with about-faces and preemptory changes in organizational policy, and failing to get their input on work procedures that affect them. It involves as well the "layoff/rehire" cycle common in many industries and organizations. Depending on the size, structure, and context of the organization, its executives, managers, and supervisors will not experience these indignities, or they will experience them differently than staff who are at a different level on the organizational staircase. Regardless of position, denial of employee involvement is, in effect, the treatment of staff as chattel.

Not only do staff appreciate being involved (American culture is still very "No Taxation Without Representation," a political truism that also holds in the organization), but they often tend to have very specific local knowledge: The closer you are to a problem, the more information about it you can provide. Managers who avoid involving staff not only fail to cultivate worth and morale, but they also decline to take available information into account. But perhaps worse than *noninvolvement* is *fake involvement*, which occurs when managers have already reached a decision but ask staff for input without disclosing this.

OTHER IMPAIRMENT IN THE WORKPLACE

While Hodson is a great place to start, he far from covers the waterfront with respect to organizational wrongdoing and the organizational impairment of human dignity. A number of additional problematic issues emerge from the literature.

Rascally Coworkers

In American professional culture, staff like to "get along" with colleagues, regardless of relative position on the organizational staircase—although there is no expectation that colleagues must be close personal friends. Coworkers who exhibit hostility, are pushy or deceitful, or are rude and egotistical can make life hell at work. Difficult coworkers can cause tremendous workplace distress. Solomon's categories and my responses, listed previously, are also helpful here.

Opacity

Opacity is the opposite of transparency in the workplace. Directly contrary to "What you see is what you get," an opaque workplace is characterized by "Nothing is as it seems." Its hallmarks are secret deals, hidden arrangements, off-the-books compensation, and so on. In an opaque work environment, staff often encounter undiscussed, unresolved emotional fallout from earlier conflict and implicit institutional memory/traditions. The result can be confusion over what is true or real in the organization (ranging from topics as weighty as who is really in charge to those as mundane as why we really don't hang pictures with nails). In more extreme instances, it can create a sense of danger and trepidation, akin to walking through a minefield (the real rules of the organization aren't revealed until you break one and it blows up).

Generational Differences

Though often over- or underemphasized, generational differences in the workplace can lead to miscommunication, misunderstanding, conflict, and reduced productivity. This is not a new problem (remember the 1960s?), though at present three distinct, and very different, generations occupy center stage in the American workforce. These include Baby Boomers (born 1946–1964), Gen Xers (1965–1980), and Millennials (1981–1999). On the wings are Traditionals (pre-1945) and GenZ (2000 or later).

Distinctions emerge in several fundamental categories. A recent Robert Half (2017) survey of CFOs indicates that executives view communication skills, adapting to change, technical skills, and cross-departmental collaboration as major areas of difference among generations. Specifically, Baby Boomers, despite their countercultural youth, tend to communicate in a more reserved fashion and prefer hierarchical management approaches. Younger workers are more comfortable with collaboration and coaching. Moreover, younger workers see change as "a vehicle for new opportunities" or simply a fact of life. Baby Boomers, however, have weathered the cultural transition from stable career environment to a more shifting and fluid experience. Thus change may be less expected and more threatening. As expected, younger workers, or "digital natives," adapt more rapidly to technological shifts and find it easier to independently upskill (Lipman, 2017).

Illness

Bona fide behavioral, physical, and mental health issues are, or contribute to, very complex, difficult-to-navigate organizational problems. First, the desire to help the person in the sick role conflicts with the need for that staff member's responsibilities to be carried out. Second, ill individuals, for a variety of understandable reasons, often hide or deny their illness, delay seeking treatment, and amplify the ramifications. When the boss is ill—and, even worse, when he or she is untreated—consequences mushroom. Responsibilities that a boss should be undertaking, such as providing consistent, careful strategic direction and making strategic decisions, are deferred, delayed, or distracted, and adversely affect the organization's culture, mission, and implementation capacities.

Exit, Voice, and Loyalty

What can one do when confronted with any one of these problems or a combination of them? That question was answered by economist Albert O. Hirschman (2004) in *Exit, Voice, and Loyalty: Responses to Declines in Forms, Organizations, and States*. When confronted with a toxic culture, or other problematic situation, Hirschman suggests, one can quit or flee (exit) speak up (voice), or remain quiet and endure it (loyalty). Many writers have emphasized exit and voice, but Hirschman himself stressed loyalty, especially its problematic aspects. Many years ago I had the opportunity to spend an afternoon with Hirschman at the Institute for Advanced Study at Princeton. We discussed this book, among other topics, and he felt that loyalty was most common and deeply problematic. He referred to Nazi Germany as a powerful personal example, but we touched on less expansive, less dramatic examples, such as staying in a deteriorating marriage, tolerating social exploitation at the workplace, or taking advantage of the organizational position to rip off customers. (Hewlett-Packard, for example, changes the cartridges on upgraded printers so the ones you have already purchased cannot be used.)

CONCLUSION

In this chapter we sketched out how varied social science disciplines approach organizations; surveyed major thinkers' concepts of *organization*; discussed formal and informal organizational elements and task and process foci of organizations; and explored a few organizational pathologies which, left untreated, can produce disastrous consequences. In the following chapter, we use this foundation to examine major theorists' perspectives on how organizations are structured, as well as some recent developments in organizational culture.

REFLECTION

- All organizations have a dark side. Using the topics discussed in this chapter, reflect on how yours cultivates or impairs dignity among its staff.
- How would you describe the formal aspects of your organizational culture? the informal aspects? How divergent are the two? Are there any points at which they overlap?
- In the context of your organization, do you agree with Edwards Deming's observation that 85% of what the organization produces is organization-driven and only 15% can be attributed to individual action? in other words, that organizational structure matters because it is largely the organization and its structure, rather than individuals within it, that produce (or don't produce) the results we hope to achieve? Why does this hold true (or not) in your observation?

FURTHER READING

Argyris, C. (1985). *Strategy, change and defensive routines.* Boston, MA: Pittman, 1985. (Now out of print but a seminal work on management and change)

Hodson, R. (2001). *Dignity at work.* New York, NY: Cambridge University Press. (See especially chapter 1, "The Four Faces of Dignity")

Manfred, F. R., de Vries, K., & Miller, D. (1991). *The neurotic organization: Diagnosing and revitalizing unhealthy companies.* New York, NY: HarperCollins.

5

Components of an Organization

INTRODUCTION

The organization is a social reality *sui generis,* or "of itself." It has a character, a culture, and a style, if you will. Likewise, orchestras perform in distinct ways, even though players, conductors, and scores differ, and restaurants prepare certain dishes well—and others not so well. (Word gets around: You want a good steak? Go here. Fish? Go there.) Community benefit organizations also have a certain style and approach, because they enact and reproduce their skills. Consider the following experiment as an illustration:

> Four chimps were put into a cage with a large bunch of bananas hanging from the top of the cage. A pole rose from the bottom of the cage to the banana bunch. One of the chimps immediately began climbing the pole to retrieve the food. As he neared the top a jet of ice water shot out at him. He tried a couple more times with the same result. He soon gave up seeking the bananas. Others intermittently tried it with the same result. Soon none of them bothered about the bananas any more. Then one chimp was removed and a "naive" chimp introduced. He immediately started up the pole but was pulled back by the other chimps. After a few more tries and a few restraints, he gave up. Over the course of the next weeks the remaining three were swapped out for new chimps. By the end none of the original chimps were there, and none of them tried to get the bananas. And none of them probably knew why (Michalko, 2012).

Now that is organization! Sometimes what we produce and reproduce in organizations is excellent. Sometimes it is not so good. But it does have a life of its own. And it is in this life-of-its-own context that managers work. (Indeed, managers play an important teaching role that enables organizations to reproduce their skills; they must take their "teacher" jobs very seriously.) When we think of organizations, we often think of the entire structural and functional unit.

We need to be aware of the whole organization, of course. But the whole is comprised of levels and parts that are as important as—perhaps even more important than—the whole, since different protocols and competencies might be required in different parts, a reality obscured when thinking of organizations as a whole. When we think of a restaurant we think of, well, the restaurant. We do not typically think of the kitchen, the wine cellar, the waiter staff, and the management and leadership as distinct parts of the restaurant (though food critics surely do, and food magazines do as well).

Three organizational thinkers—Talcott Parsons, Henry Mintzberg, and Tom Peters—have developed perspectives on organizational parts and elements that are extremely helpful to managers and leaders. Parsons (1960) discusses levels of organizations; Mintzberg (1989) describes parts of the organizations; and Peters (1982) talks about changes in organizational dynamics and presentation to cope with pressures of cultural speed and fluidity.

THE THREE-PART VIEW OF TALCOTT PARSONS

In his (off-puttingly titled) essay, "Some Ingredients of a General Theory of Formal Organization," sociologist Talcott Parsons (1960) introduced the idea of the organization with three levels: technical, managerial, and institutional. I summarize this view next but split Parsons' *institutional* level into *executive* and *regulatory* levels.

Technical Level

The technical level does the work of the organization. People staffing this level include caseworkers, cooks and waiters, musicians, teachers, professors, police officers working a beat, and so on. They are sometimes called "front room" staff, and they are the denominator of the "back room/front room" ratio, or the number of support people per worker needed by an organization. Key competencies here are substantive skills in actually doing the work of the organization.

Managerial Level

At the managerial level, Parsons identifies two essential managerial functions. First, the people staffing this level mediate between the technical organization and personnel and its customers (clients, students, and audience). Second, they provide the resources necessary to do the actual job (money, space, etc.).

Institutional Level

The institutional level contains the CEO and top team on the organizational side and the board of directors and other regulatory bodies that direct the organization on the regulatory side. The problem with grouping these together is that the top team, the executives, interact with the organization in a senior manager's capacity, while the board and regulatory elements exert overall control of and set direction for the organization. Let's consider each group separately.

EXECUTIVE LEVEL

The executive level contains the CEO, COO, CFO, CIO, CHRO (chief human resources officer), and any other chiefs that form the cabinet, executive committee, or top operating group. If the organization is shaped like an hourglass, they function at the "neck" of the hourglass: The organization spreads out below them and the larger community and society spread out above them. Their job is to lead and manage so that mission, vision, and values are directed to the organization in the form of guidance and to the community and society in the form of motivation to provide support and resources.

REGULATORY LEVEL

The regulatory level contains the board of directors and other bodies and organizations that control or impact the organization. Examples of the latter include accrediting bodies, government, and media.

What Does It Mean?

This four-part schema makes a few things very clear. First, the organization has a "fuzzy" bottom (customers, consumers, clients, etc.) and a "fuzzy" top (boards and regulatory bodies), a point that is illustrated in Figure 5.1. Second, the constellation of competencies (knowledge and skill) between any two levels is very different. As you rise within a level, you become better at that level's core competency. However, when you reach the top of the level, you cross a boundary into a new set of core competencies. You keep the older competencies as perspective, not for day-to-day operational use. If a physician (technical level) moves from providing patient care to hospital administration (managerial level), the competency of patient care—which was key at the technical level—is minimal. Instead, managerial tasks, the core competency in the new level, take precedence. Your growth within a level is *transactional change* (improvement) within the system; when you move from one level to another, change between levels is *transformational* or a change in the system.

As Parsons describes the organization, it is not really one entity but several (three in his original description, four in my amended one) stacked on top of one another. This four-in-one concept might take time to solidify, but it is worth the investment, since it provides a timeless overview of levels and their functions.

THE SIX-PART VIEW OF HENRY MINTZBERG

Mintzberg (1989) also conceptualizes organizations as comprised of parts, albeit more complex than Parsons' model. Perhaps a better way to think about
Mintzberg's insight is 5 + 1. The five parts of the organization are outlined in
Figure 5.1. The entire organization is contained within or bound by ideology or
values. The central "stack" has three parts, similar to Parsons'. At the bottom is
the *operating core,* which corresponds to Parsons' technical level. In the middle
is the *middle line,* which aligns with Parsons' managerial level. At the top is the
strategic apex, analogous to the executive level in my reformulation of Parsons
(see Figure 5.1).

   Mintzberg adds two sidebars that stand as giant eggs on either side of the stack.
One is the *techno structure,* and the other is the *support staff.* There are spaces between the two eggs and the rest of the organization, suggesting that, while part of
the same package, they have a certain degree of organizational independence. That
is why I added the two sets of double lines between operating core and middle line
and between the middle line and the strategic apex. Mintzberg did not provide
that separation in his original diagram, but it follows the suggested separation of

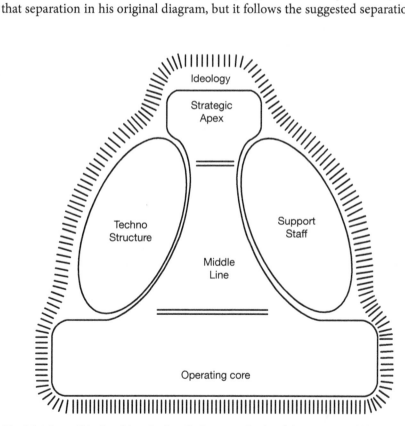

*For Mintzberg, "ideology" is not a "part" of an organization, it is a context within which the
organization operates and which, in one or another ways, suffuses each of the parts.

Figure 5.1 Four levels of the organization.

techno structure and support staff. What Mintzberg calls *ideology* (a strong term) we might call *culture* or *values*.

TOM PETERS' NEWER AND OLDER MODELS OF ORGANIZATIONS

Tom Peters is one of the most creative contemporary thinkers on organizations. While he earned a PhD in organizational behavior, Peters, unlike Parsons and Mintzberg, works outside of the academy, garnering broad exposure that, I think, works in his favor. Like Parsons, Peters is interested in the way an organization responds to its environment. Like Mintzberg, he sees the organization as "encapsulated" (more so in the older model than the newer one).

In Figures 5.2 and 5.3 Peters describes his older and newer models of organization (Peters & Waterman, 1982). In the "Inflexible, Rule Determined Mass Producer of the Past" there is a thick boundary separating the internal organization and the outside organization; it was hard to get in, but once you were in, you were in. This might be a combination of Quinn's (1988) clan and hierarchy models (see chapter 4). Insulation continues into the very center of the organization. The executive core is exceptionally well insulated and is a great distance from Parsons' customers and controllers. If uncertainty absorption (see chapter 2) exists in any organization it is here, because information is very "processed" by the time it gets to the boss.

Peters' newer organizational model is nimble and open. Its thin lines suggest permeable boundaries. Indeed it is difficult to be sure who is or is not a "member" of the organization, because those with various kinds of relationships to it (customers and suppliers are seen inside the organization, and employees are "outside," working with customers and consumers). It is the boundary-less organization, something of a blend of Quinn's (1988) adhocracy and market models.

Peters' diagrams in essence refer to the "whole" organization, and they are useful in that way. While no organization exactly follows either, we could locate ourselves in an organizational "space" defined by his dimensions. If we use his dimensions, we have a table something like the one in Figure 5.4. The figure assumes that all organizations have properties of the variables, rather than wholly occupying one or the other.

THE ORGANIZATIONAL CIRCLE

Peters' illustrations are evocative in another way. Organizations are almost always rendered in the box-and-line mode known as the organizational chart. CEO at the top, VPs one level down, department directors below that, and so on. The organizational chart has become emblematic of hierarchical authority, of who

What Have Things Been Like?
Tom Peters Tell Us*

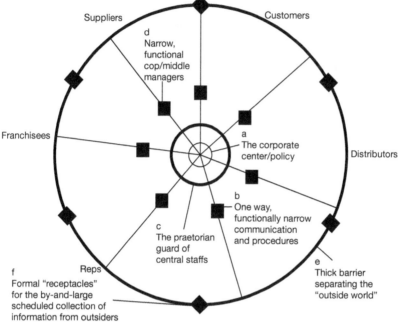

**The Inflexible, Rule-determined,
Mass Producer of the Past: All Persons Know Their Place**

Start with (a), the corporate center/policy. This is the traditional, invisible, impersonal, generally out-of-touch corporate hub. The tininess of the circle representing the corporate center suggests both tightness and narrowness of scope; communication to the outside world (in or beyond the firm's official boundary) is usually via formal declaration — — the policy manual or the multivolume plan, by and large determined on hgh—and communicated via the chain of command (i.e., downward). Within this tiny circle lie the "brains of the organization." It is here, almost exclusively, that the long-term thinking, planning, and peering into the future take place.

*Tom peters, "Restoring American Competitiveness: Looking for New Models of Organizations," **Academy of Management Executives**, 2,2 (may 1988): 103–107.

Figure 5.2 What have things been like? Tom Peters tells us.

is "over" whom and who "reports to" whom. Because it is assembled by level, meeting with someone who is not your supervisor or manager but who is the manager's manager is viewed by a hierarchical organization as improper—as a skip-level meeting. These usually trigger a range of consequences, since they violate hierarchical norms.

Peters' circles invite us to think of other ways to render organizational relationships, ways that have inherent order in and regularity to them. Thinking about the organization as a solar system or as an atom has some value. In this

So What's New?
Tom Again*

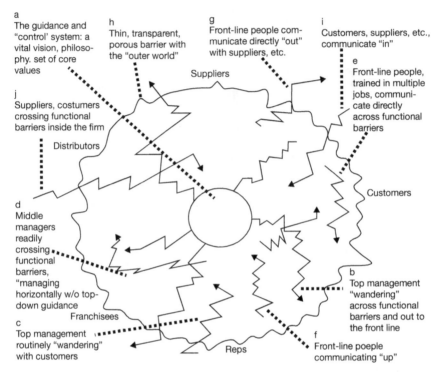

a
The guidance and "control' system: a vital vision, philosophy. set of core values

h
Thin, transparent, porous barrier with the "outer world"

g
Front-line people communicate directly "out" with suppliers, etc.

i
Customers, suppliers, etc., communicate "in"

Suppliers

e
Front-line people, trained in multiple jobs, communicate directly across functional barriers

j
Suppliers, costumers crossing functional barriers inside the firm

Distributors

Customers

d
Middle managers readily crossing functional barriers, "managing horizontally w/o top-down guidance

Franchisees

b
Top management "wandering" across functional barriers and out to the front line

c
Top management routinely "wandering" with customers

Reps

f
Front-line poeple communicating "up"

The Flexible, Porous, Adaptive, Fleet-of-Foot Organization of the Future: Every Person is " Paid" to be Obstreperous, a Disrespecter of Formal Boundaries, to Hustle and to Be Engaged Fully with Engendering Swift Actions,

*Tom Peters, "Restoring American Competitiveness: Looking for New Models of Organization," **Academy of Management Executives**, 2,2 (May 1988): 103-107.

Figure 5.3 So what's new? Tom again.

rendering (see Figure 5.4), departments orbit executive positions, rather than being beneath them. The executive then becomes central to, rather than over, them. This concept suggests changes to the structure and nature of organizational and hierarchical relationships. The solar system model (Figure 5.4) also means that only "orbits" not "levels" are crossed, giving the executive better access to all parts of the organization. It also suggests healthy, nonchaotic dynamism and changing of positions, rather than stasis.

In the atom rendition (Figure 5.4b), orbits are elliptical and departments have positions both close to and far from the executive core. Such variability is good. If a department is too close to the executive core it can be co-opted by that view. On the other hand, if a department is too far from the center of the organization, the executive core loses awareness and supportive views. Hence a "now-closer-now-further" dynamic can work very well.

(a)

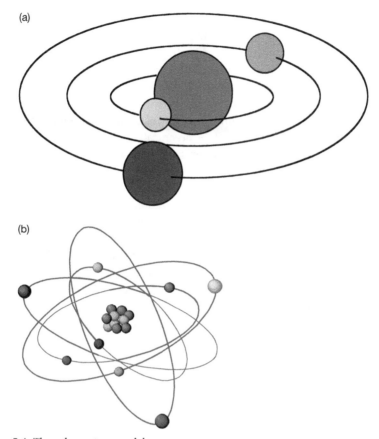

(b)

Figure 5.4 The solar system model.

There are other ways to think about organizations as well. One CEO whom I interviewed argued for the pizza model of organizations. In the pizza model, dough underlies everything. Given the importance of money to organizations, that is not so farfetched. Crust thickness refers to the richness of resources the organization can access. Overlying the crust is "the big cheese" or executive. Other positions are occupied by big pepperonis, little pepperonis, olives, mushrooms, or whatever, all as parts of the organizational pizza. In a funny way, it works.

ORGANIZATIONS AS A MATRIX OF PERMISSION AND CONTROL

Organizations are most often seen as control structures. Much organizational activity emphasizes this aspect of their functioning. *Reporting relationships, lines of authority,* and other concepts stress organizational control. Indeed, conventional understandings of managing and supervising convey a sense of superior-subordinate, more power-less power relationships. The sociological literature is full of books and courses on *social control*, those formal and informal social and cultural strictures that limit, direct, and prescribe acceptable behavior. While social control is the larger context of organizational control, managers not only control; they also permit. Hence, you might think (as I do), that social control has received too much emphasis, to the extent that it ignores *social permission*, or the "okaying" of a whole range of behavioral repertoires.

Like social control, social permission also exists within organizations, and its expression shapes (and is shaped by) the organizations. For example, an organization may "okay" dark practices that impair dignity of staff and organization, such as using office supplies for personal purposes, padding expense accounts, nepotistic hiring and lack of firing, and sexual relationships in or related to the workplace. Often, formally, the very same organization would deny any connection with such practices. But social permission in an organization is often implicit, and information about it is transferred informally. As a result, deniability is possible. However, not all social permission is destructive. Organizations can shape, or be shaped by, positive expressions of permission such as the ability to take official time for philanthropic work, economy and flexibility of means while retaining stability of ends, and flexible work time and locations.

Be aware that organizations supply both control and permission. To see only part of the picture is to miss the richness of the organization, whether formal or informal (family, neighborhood association, etc.). We all live and work in permission and control spaces, in environments that supply both permission and controls (Tropman, 1986).

ORGANIZATIONS AND THEIR HUMAN RESOURCES

The practice of management and leadership is curiously bifurcated. On the one hand, the historic "scientific management and leadership" approach tends to see people as replaceable parts. In this view, whatever humanity staff possess is irrelevant to their function in the organization. "Our way or the highway" is a suitable mantra for this view, and *span of control*, or number of people you can actually observe and check, is a key element. That number is, well, five. Given the importance of span of control, it is no wonder that organizations who adopted the scientific approach grew tall and pointy. At every step on the organizational staircase, leaders managed five direct reports.

The "human factor" of organizations came into prominence after 1945, and people (as people) became more important within the organization; In part, this emergence of "the human factor" came about because of World War II. Personnel departments morphed into human resources departments. Human factors became seen as organizations' "greatest resources." In this view, span of control, mentioned earlier, is supplanted by *span of communication*. In this model, supervisors and managers oversee many more than five people because they do not have to check the work of each person. Employees check their own work and go to the supervisor for help if and as needed. The magical 5 became 50. Managers supervise 5 within the span of control but resource 50 if they work within a span of communication.

Of course, as span of control shifted to span of communication, organizational direction moved from external to internal, and social permission also increased. These changes required not only technical skills on the part of staff but judgment as well. Criteria became less concrete, and simultaneous mutual feedback, as we experience when driving in traffic, became the norm. The manager became less overseer and more guide, but the structure and content of jobs changed faster, generally, than managers adapted.

For the reasons just mentioned, communication, interpersonal skills, and group process skills became more important. Most seemed to agree that managers needed these skills, but it was somewhat unclear exactly what actually were "good" communication, interpersonal skills and group process skills. Certainly, there are technical elements to each, such as effective listening, clear use of language, communication using more than one medium (e.g., speaking and writing or speaking and having video or audio backup). Seminars in "supportive communication," "active listening," and tests on "communication styles" are now a mainstay of managerial training at most executive education centers.

Emotional Management and Leadership in the Workplace

As organizations began to take a more human, less assembly-line view of employees, it took some time before they recognized—and began to manage and lead as if—emotions are part of the humanness employees bring to the workplace. As a sociologist of emotions, Arlie Russell Hochschild has pioneered the study of emotional labor in a commercial setting. Hochschild examines the culture of emotional display rules; surface and deep emotion; and emotion, work, and management. Hochschild's (1983) groundbreaking *The Managed Heart* reports on a qualitative study of flight attendants and the emotional labor they exert to apparently effortlessly manage *irates,* passengers who are angry, offensive, or inappropriate and who cannot exit the plane. She examines how flight attendants, and employees in other aspects of the service industry, learn to recognize and manage feelings. In the process she developed the theory of the workplace as a sea of emotions and feelings. Organizations, she observes, have developed ways (largely unacknowledged and largely done by women) to "manage" (address, respond to, and accommodate) these feelings.

Everyone appreciates "process-focused" employees in whom others can confide, who arrange monthly birthday celebrations, who make the workplace a colorful and pleasant place to work. Until recently these efforts were considered sidebars, nice add-ons to the "real" work of an organization; job descriptions certainly did not include being nice and bringing flowers to the office. However, managing feelings and emotions is now recognized as a core managerial and leadership competency. Managing in this context means recognizing the emotionality of situations, responding appropriately to the expressing of feeling, encouraging *affect control* (the channeling of appropriate feeling into constructive pathways), and dealing especially with anger—your own and others'.

Following Hochschild, Goleman (1995) launched the emotional intelligence movement with his *Emotional Intelligence*. This book and the work it inspired spurred the effort to understand emotional management and leadership in the workplace. In the emotional intelligence framework, EQ is even more important than IQ in understanding organizational and personal success and failure. Emotional intelligence in the workplace incorporates understanding and practice of *self-awareness,* knowing what you feel when you feel it; *management and leadership of feelings,* the ability to control impulses, soothe anxiety, and experience appropriate anger; *motivation,* zeal, persistence, and optimism in the face of setbacks; *empathy,* the ability to read and respond to unspoken feelings; and *social skills,* the ability to handle the emotional reactions of others, to interact with, smooth, and manage relationships. These qualities may be manifested, respectively, with realistic self-assessment; being comfortable with ambiguity and open to change; maintaining optimism despite failure and a commitment to achieve; cultivating expertise in building/retaining talent, exercising sensitivity, and serving clients; and effectively leading change, persuading without manipulating, and building and leading teams.

CONCLUSION

In this chapter and in our discussion of Quinn (see chapter 4), we examined organizational models that help us see how managerial work (surveyed in chapters 2 and 3) is heavily influenced by the settings in which that work takes place. They offer us several insights. First, organizations have identifiable structural and cultural features. Quinn's (1988) cultural focus encourages us to look around and see what kind of organization we are working in. This is an important focus, but there are also others. While many aspects of management and leadership and supervision are common across all venues, there are differences in the pace, expectations, demand schedule, and outcome measures that managers and leaders must take into account.

Second, Parsons (1960) highlights the "fuzzy" edges of the organization of both input and output, where clients, consumers, customers, vendors, and others influence us. Managers often connect with those outside the organization, and they need to keep their organizational requirements and demands in mind as they do. One aspect of managerial work is clarifying and structuring—then reclarifying and restructuring—these "fuzzy" relationships. Parsons also highlights the control that regulatory and governing bodies exercise over the organization (these are "fuzzy" as well), the relative independence of levels within the organization, and the distinct competencies required of each level.

Third, Mintzberg (1989) stresses the uniqueness and autonomy of the organizational parts. Though he does picture the whole organization as surrounded by a net of ideology, or culture (more fuzziness), his central insight about intraorganizational uniqueness is robust. My work on the organizational circle and other ways of conceptualizing and displaying organizations is useful as another way to draw and to think about your organization.

And, finally, Hochschild (1983) and Goleman (1995) add a human element to management and leadership with their work on emotions in organizations and emotional management and leadership as an essential managerial competency.

The discussions in this chapter refer to all organizations. However, community benefit organizations have distinctive features and challenges. It is to these that we now turn.

REFLECTION

Understanding Your Organization
- On a sheet of paper, using the models we reviewed (Quinn, Parsons, Peters, Mintzberg, Tropman), identify your organization's primary features.
- Try locating your organization in Peters' space.
- Try this exercise in a staff meeting, even if you find these metaphors a bit of a stretch. See if teams of staff could actually draw the organization as a circle, or an atom, or a pizza. Then think about how relationships might change as a result.

Emotions at Work
- Take a few minutes to think, independently or in conversation, about how emotions are managed in your workplace. What expression of emotion is permitted? What unexpressed undercurrents affect the work environment?
- How do managers and leaders explicitly engage emotions—whether staff bring them to work or whether they arise as a result of circumstances at work?

FURTHER READING

Goleman, D. (2005). *Emotional intelligence: Why it can matter more than IQ.* New York, NY: Bantam.

Hochschild, A. (2012). *The managed heart: The commercialization of human feeling* (3rd ed.). Berkeley: University of California Press.

Mintzberg, H. (2007). *Mintzberg on management: Inside our strange world of organizations.* New York, NY: Free Press.

Mintzberg, H. (2013). *Simply managing.* Oakland, CA: Berrett-Koehler.

Peters, T., & Waterman., R. (2006). *In search of excellence: Lessons from America's best-run companies.* New York, NY: HarperBusiness.

6

Community Benefit Organizations

INTRODUCTION

As we've established in chapters 4 and 5, organizations, despite differing sectors, sizes, and functions, have much in common. In fact, distinctions among organizations often depend less on differences in sector and more on those in size. The University of Michigan, for example, is a nonprofit organization with an annual budget of more than $7 billion. Some storefront nonprofits have only one employee, and many community organizations have no employees at all, fueled instead by volunteer time and energy. The same is true in the corporate sector, which ranges from large public companies like General Electric and private companies like Cargill to mom-and-pop organizations and sole proprietorships. In the government sector, organizations run from the Executive Office of the president of the United States to small municipal and village operations; school districts; water districts; library districts, and so on.

In terms of function, almost no organization operates in the purview of only one sector. For example, healthcare—whether gerontological care, substance abuse, or counseling—is delivered by government, corporate, and community benefit entities. Moreover, care is influenced by all of these sectors, regardless of which type of organization delivers it. (Healthcare is regulated by all levels of government. Its services are often contracted to for-profit vendors and mediated by for-profit insurance companies. It may be delivered or administrated by a nonprofit organization.) These commonalities make the manager's job a puzzlement. Does it matter whether you practice in a county hospital, a privately held corporation, or a community benefit organization? Does it matter who takes care of you when your health is at risk? The answer is it does, but perhaps not as much as it used to.

A FOCUS ON WICKED PROBLEMS

Regardless of size, sector, history, or function, community benefit organizations tend to share a focus on what Rittel and Webber (1973) called *wicked problems.* In their formulation, *wicked* refers to complexity rather than ethical behavior. Pioneered as a social policy concept, the term has been widely adopted, applied, and interpreted. It commonly refers to a social or cultural problem that is difficult or impossible to solve due to incomplete or contradictory knowledge, the number of people and opinions involved, the large economic burden engendered, and the interconnected nature of wicked problems with other problems. Rittel and Webber identify common features of wicked problems as:

1. No definitive formulation.
2. No criteria for determining when the problem is solved.
3. Solutions can be only good/bad, not true/false.
4. No test for whether a proposed solution is a good one.
5. Every solution is a "one-shot" operation. Implementing it makes irreversible changes.
6. There is no exhaustive set of possible solutions or permissible operations.
7. Every wicked problem is unique.
8. Every wicked problem can be a symptom of another problem.
9. People choose explanations for wicked problems that seem plausible to them. Their solutions are shaped by their explanations.
10. Planners have the right to be wrong (but they must take responsibility for their actions).

Most social problems—inequality, political instability, death, disease, or famine—are wicked.

Wicked problems can't be "fixed," but they can be mitigated, and this is the knotty, thorny mission that community benefit organizations undertake.

AMERICAN NEGATIVITY TO SOCIAL HELPING

Wicked problems have been exacerbated in American society by a strong emphasis on independence and a cultural ambivalence toward collective social helping—both giving and receiving it.

And despite a thriving philanthropic sector and a strong cultural emphasis on duty and responsibility, American society has often been hostile to helping those in need—a hostility that ranges from early to contemporary policy. Among these, social scientists number President Franklin Pierce's 1854 veto of the "bill for the indigent insane," an initiative to create asylums for the mentally ill spearheaded by Dorothea Dix and passed by both houses of Congress; the phasing out of Civil War Pensions; and the 1872 closure of the Freedman's Bureau (DuBois, 1901, VCU Libraries Social Welfare History Project, n.d.). The Nichols Plan, advanced by John Nichols in Oklahoma in the mid-1930s and of interest to President Roosevelt's advisor Colonel Woods, illustrates the tension regarding aid in American social policy:

> Thus John B. Nichols of the Oklahoma Gas Utilities Company wrote to his friend Patrick J. Hurley, the Secretary of War, about an idea he was trying out in Chickasha, Oklahoma. By the Nichols plan, restaurants were asked to dump food left on plates into five-gallon containers; the unemployed could qualify for these scraps by chopping wood donated by farmers. "We expect a little trouble now and then from those who are not worthy of the support of the citizens," Nichols wrote philosophically, "but we must contend with such cases in order to take care of those who are worthy." (Schlessinger, 1957, p. 179)

Americans continue to grapple with the fear that the needy will "rip us off." As but one example, DeSmet (1992) published a column in a Detroit newspaper reporting:

> The Central Business District Association recently handed out 1,200 flyers in Detroit asking people to stop giving money to panhandlers. "Avoid supporting what in most cases is an alcoholic and destructive lifestyle," the posters say. "You need not feel guilty when saying no."

Attaining acceptance for social helping has been an uphill battle in America. (It was reviewing these problems that inspired me to write *Does America Hate the Poor?*) In fact, this fear of being ripped off controverts Pope Francis' recent exhortation to give to the homeless without concern for how they spend it (O'Loughlin, 2017).

So regardless of the sector in which a community benefit organization is situated, its staff are likely to encounter a range of wicked problems, ambivalent attitudes toward social helping, and complexities that stem from taking on wicked problems in an ambivalent context.

Assessing the Scope of the Community Benefit Sector in the United States

Before we consider the community benefit organization's characteristics and problems, however, let's get a sense of identity and scope. We've already established that the term *community benefit organization* is more apt than *nonprofit*, since it incorporates all prosocial groups. The historical social agency can also be called the public/private social service organization. I suggest this name because they have two sources of public support: "tax expenditure" received by tax status and tax relief available to those who give charitable deductions. To my thinking, most of the agencies we are discussing here have forgotten those civic supports. Just how substantial is the sector? (For the sake of available data, we'll need to restrict our inquiry to the nonprofit sector only, rather than including corporate and public prosocial helping organizations. If we did include them, the figures reported here would be much larger. I am using the term *nonprofit* here because the Charity Navigator looks at organizations in this tax status. If we were to add corporate and public prosocial helping organizations, the figure would be much greater.)

The nonprofit sector is, well, large. The following figures regarding the nonprofit sector are from the National Center for Charitable Statistics:

1,571,056 tax-exempt organizations:

- 1,097,689 public charities
- 105,030 private foundations
- 368,337 other types of nonprofit organizations, including chambers of commerce, fraternal organizations and civic leagues (NCCS Data Archive, n.d.).

Public Charity Finances

In 2013, public charities reported over $1.74 trillion in total revenues and $1.63 trillion in total expenses. Of the revenue:

- 21% came from contributions, gifts, and government grants.
- 72% came from program service revenues, which include government fees and contracts.
- 7% came from "other" sources including dues, rental income, special event income, and gains or losses from goods sold (NCCS Data Archive, n.d.).

Public Charity Assets
   Public charities reported over $3 trillion in total assets in 2013 (NCCS Data Archive, n.d.).

PROBLEMS IN AND SOLUTIONS FOR COMMUNITY BENEFIT ORGANIZATIONS

The mission of community benefit organizations is vital to the well-being of our fellow humans and to the health of our society. Sometimes it can be rewarding—if the workplace itself is structured to nourish staff despite the Sisyphean presence of wicked problems. In this context, managers and leaders, regardless of position, encounter a constellation of challenges that is endemic, if not unique, to the community benefit organization—a constellation that further complicates efforts to address and mitigate wicked problems. You would think that these pressures would cause managers and leaders to prioritize outstanding management, avoidance of burnout, and wise efforts to shepherd and increase resources. However, all too often, these organizations are undermanaged and underled (NCCS Data Archive, n.d.); the workloads contribute to burnout; and the compensation does not begin to approach effort invested. Looking at the sector and understanding it is a crucial step toward urgently needed excellent management and leadership. In the next section, I list problems that community benefit organizations face and potential remedies with which managers and leaders can begin.

Problem: Boards of Directors Are Deeply Flawed

Boards underperform and perform incorrectly in several areas. Some of these difficulties are reflected in nomenclature. Members are usually called *board members,* a nondescript term that has no particular function or history assigned to it. I recommend "trustees," which emphasizes the responsibility of stewardship and reinforces that "it is not their money," something easily and often forgotten if you are not the donor who gave the money.

As Frumkin (2002) notes, there is little external or internal accountability. Other than the board itself, community benefit organizations have few external controls, although there have been some congressional moves in that direction, especially with foundations and expenditure rates to avoid financial warehousing. Similarly, boards have limited across-the-board operational standards. The Independent Sector (2016) proposed some a few years ago, but adoption has been limited.

Of course boards have their own bylaws, but there is wide variance in their operationalization in, for example, trustee tenure. I have often worked with boards that are not in compliance with their bylaws, having members sitting for two or three terms past their allowed time frame because no one has the courage to tell them to move on. Another example is CEO review. It is frequently semi- to nonexistent, or done with a lick and a promise. In other instances, trustees have no idea what they are to do individually and collectively; their processes and meetings become a venue for expressing and implementing private agendas; and they are typically run by the most socially powerful person on the board. Singly and severally, these problems create what Deming (1982) called *incalculable loss,* an immeasurably huge—and often unrecognized—cost.

Remedies

This situation is beginning to change in the United States. Board Source (formerly the National Center for Nonprofit Boards) offers consulting and training services for community benefit organizations (BoardSource, n.d.). However, an overhaul of boards is needed.

1. In the United States, nonprofits are publicly supported organizations, relieved of tax burdens. All boards should, therefore, account to the public for the accomplishments and trials of their organizations each year.
2. All board members/directors/trustees should be trained in proper board responsibilities and deportment. The organization is not their plaything.
3. Every board should evaluate itself and each director every year.
4. Each board should have a strategic plan that is posted on its website (of course that means the organization needs a website). There should be job descriptions for each board position, from member through chairperson, so that expectations are clear.
5. Each year, every director should be required, as a part of continuation, to take part in one new training event.

Problem: Managers, Executive Directors, and the Top Team Are Often Untrained or Poorly Trained at the Front End

Managers, executives, and C-level teams are surrounded by high and often unexpressed expectations. Praise is meager, criticism voluminous. In the community benefit sector they are also, by and large, untrained in management and leadership competencies, and continuing education programs are few.

They are also mal-trained. In the absence of formation for an executive or senior position, they use the skills of their last position, assuming they are appropriate for the new one. Frequently, an excellent technical staff member (recall Parsons' levels of the organization: technical, managerial, executive/regulatory, discussed in chapter 5) is promoted to the managerial level. This promotion is based upon the assumption, held by promoters and promotees, that the new position is an extension of, rather than different from, the old one.

However, being good at your old position may disqualify you for your new position, because what you're good at becomes your default style and, under stress (which is practically synonymous with a new position), you are more likely to resort to that default style. An early diagnostic version of this phenomenon emerged as "The Peter Principle," which sought to explain why so many managers were incompetent (Peter & Hull, 2011). Peter observed that organizations structured incompetence by promoting employees until they reached their level of incompetence. There they remain.

Remedies

But progress is on the horizon. For example, the Amherst Wilder Foundation in Minneapolis has taken a leadership role in making "easy to use materials" available to executives and their staffs in a variety of key areas. But what practical steps can organizations take to improve the situation?

1. Require managerial training, not just experience, to be part of a candidate's portfolio.
2. Begin a process that requires training of executives and top team members.
3. As a hiring committee or board, make a plan to train and mentor new executives and senior managers. (Nonprofit management and leadership is a growth area in American higher education, as the recent proliferation of certificate- and continuing education–level programs demonstrates. Centers for nonprofit management and leadership around the United States (Indiana University, Case Western Reserve University, and others) are under vigorous development, and local and regional communities are supporting the development of training and standards organizations like the Charlottesville, Virginia, Center for Nonprofit Excellence. But the need is still great.
4. The strategic plan should provide the basis for the annual plan that the executive director (CEO/CPO) carries out. It should be the responsibility of the executive committee to see that such a plan is in place, and that it is connected to the evaluation of the executive director/CEO/CPO.
5. Executives need to develop a career path for themselves and need assistance in doing so. Training *after* hire and *during* tenure should be present, just as board training is present. If the organization does not provide continuing educational opportunities, it is worthwhile for middle managers, project managers, and supervisory managers to seek out opportunities on their own.

Problem: Fiscal Knowledge Is Limited

The limited training executives and future executives do receive for executive and managerial roles is shy on financial management skills, including accounting. No respectable research program would omit a statistics course, but few nonprofit management and leadership training programs include an accounting course.

Remedies

Offer regular training in fiscal management and leadership for nonprofit staff and managers. Detroit's Accounting Aid Society (not the best name, perhaps, but an excellent idea) began helping individuals and organizations with taxes and book-keeping and now provides a range of training opportunities for nonprofit staff in fiscal and other areas (Accounting Aid Society, n.d.). Every city or region should have access to a similar organization.

Problem: The Voice of the Customer (Consumer, Client) Is Largely Silent

Although evaluation, particularly of grant compliance, is a standard component of community benefit organizations, they have been slower to embrace the program and services assessment mindset for their own services. Executives, all too often, become apologists for lackluster agency performance rather than leaders down the road to better quality. Quality is driven by feedback, and feedback comes from the end user. Regretfully, robust systems for harvesting, interpreting, and implementing are the exception rather than the rule. However, such systems can help managers and staff, and organizations as a whole, improve performance.

Remedies

Each agency needs to develop its own set of internal and external customers and ask them for feedback—often and in detail. Most car dealerships (not the highest in customer service) at least give customers a card to mail in rating the service. Most community benefit organizations do not meet even this minimal standard.

Problem: Evaluation Often Measures Process, Not Impact

What are the results of human intervention? Do community benefit organizations add value, help people, or make a difference? Famous wit Dorothy Parker, when told that President Calvin Coolidge had died, is reported to have quipped, "How can they tell?" This question applies to community benefit organizations too. "Are you helping?" And "How can you tell?" Doing "good" is not enough. You need to do it right, and do it well. Evaluation and reporting have historically focused on process or output. "We had X interviews with Y clients," "we served Z number of children in our center," and so on. But does anyone get better? On *that* question we often have little to share. (Not all process or output measures are problematic: hot meals served, women given shelter, etc. are some examples.) But overall, evaluation needs to shift from output to outcome and impact.

Remedies

1. The success metrics outlined by Peter Vail and others at the beginning of this book provide some elements for evaluation criteria. Organizations must be open to the question, "Do we make a difference?" If the answer is *no*, they must be willing to change. If the answer is *yes*, then they must be willing to ask, "Does the difference we make matter?" For both

inquiries, the questions of "How do we know?" and "Is our information reliable and valid?" need to be satisfactorily addressed.

2. Some organizations serve in industries or sectors that require accreditation. And while accreditation does not solve every problem, it is a form of accountability.

3. Given the connectivity and transparency of the Internet and social media—and the implicit threat of negative publicity—community benefit organizations benefit from the accountability built into crowd-sourced and interactive platforms such as Yelp and GlassDoor.

4. Executive guides, compilations of information about community benefit organization leaders, can easily and impartially report what leaders have accomplished, what professional difficulties they had at previous organizations, and how others have experienced working with them. At present, this information exists but lacks a hub.

Problem: Consultative Help Is Available But Episodically Used

When for-profit organizations have troubles, they call upon Bain & Co, The Boston Consulting Group, McKinsey, or any number of other consulting firms to help them out. In the community benefit sector, this function is present (myself included) but is usually accessed on an episodic rather than ongoing basis. Most common are consultations involving evaluation.

But consultative resources are scarce, and often there is no budget for them as such. Managerial and executive coaching and organizational development are more rare when evaluation is not initially involved. Further, when they do occur, those involved rarely collaborate with others, so there is little "knowledge recapture." For-profit consulting firms, for example, milk the "float" of knowledge from each client to help all clients. The firms represent a storehouse of accumulated and processed knowledge about organizations, what makes them work well, what processes are useful, what kinds of things should be avoided, and so on. Hence the consultations, theoretically, improve as the interventions are based on more knowledge.

These are not the only problems that administration and management and leadership in social work agencies suffer, but they will suffice. They are among the most important from a managerial perspective. The existence of such problems singly and severally means that social work agencies, as a whole, are underled, undermanaged, and oversupervised. This situation occurs because managers and executives, shy of executive and managerial knowledge and experience, revert to their default "supervisory" experience, which often means micromanagement and leadership, inbox clearing, and paper shuffling.

Remedies

1. We need to develop consultative capacity for the community benefit sector. One example might be the Forbes Fund, a supporting organization of the Pittsburgh Foundation. Started in 1980 by my father, Elmer J. Tropman, it provided grants to help support consultants who work with nonprofits who needed help. Other communities may also have such functions under development.
2. In addition, the Forbes Fund, the Alliance for Strong Families and Communities, and other national organizations maintain consultant lists.
3. At a more fundamental level, the culture of continuous improvement and organizational development is not strongly present in the community benefit sector, especially in the nonprofit component of that sector. As mentioned earlier, the pressure of inadequate financing and the press of wicked problems tends to make professional and organizational development a low priority.

Problem: Poor Project Management Skills and Protocols

The structure and purpose of many organizations in the community benefit sector, as I just explained, make their work difficult. Let me point out here that if financing is continually inadequate, then different decision-making systems in terms of what tasks can be reasonably undertaken is needed. The very nature of that work and the expectations surrounding it can be and are deeply problematic. But not all tasks are wicked problem tasks. They may be as workaday as planning the annual meeting or organizing a fundraiser. To give one example, I worked with an agency that had an annual Thanksgiving basket program: Each Thanksgiving, donated food was procured and meal baskets shared with families that could not afford such a meal.

The executive complained to me that this task seemed to take longer every year. I discovered that no protocols, notebooks, Gantt charts, or other helps had ever been developed for this important piece of agency work. Each year, the coordinator (there was almost always a new coordinator for this negatively charged project) started from scratch and "asked around" to get a sense of the project. This practice usually resulted in a crunch, in which all staff were mobilized (along with volunteers, who complained that they had not been notified until the last minute) to get the food, sort it, package it, decide who should get it, and find out how big the families were so that an appropriate package could be put together and delivered. Everyone was too exhausted to celebrate or recognize staff and volunteers.

When I reported this situation to the executive and observed that most parent-teacher organizations do better than this with their ice cream socials, she was troubled and aghast. "What do they do?" she asked.

"Well," I replied, "they at minimum have a notebook that lists the tasks that need to be done and when, so that next year can run better than last year, not worse. They update the notebook every year with essential information, like telephone numbers, etc. And they have next year's person apprentice to this year's person."

"That would never work here," the executive replied. "We are dealing with needy people whose needs always change; we have to be sensitive to that."

"But," I pointed out, "needy or not, you provide the same product every year; you get lists from the same churches and agencies every year."

"That is the problem with you people from the university," the executive said. "You just do not know what it is like in the real world."

Needless to say my career at that agency was not an extended one.

Remedies

Make a list of work processes. Inspect each one. Develop protocols for them so that everyone is not "winging it." If your time and fiscal budgets are limited, buy a Lynda.com subscription and set up an in-house, brown-bag lunch training schedule. Or, if your budget permits, send your staff to workshops on flow charts, Gantt charts, and PERT (Program Evaluation and Review Technique).

Problem: Compensation Is Inadequate

Overall, compensation in the community benefit sector is inadequate. In some segments of the sector—healthcare and foundation work, for example—it is certainly better. But overall the pay is subpar. Additionally, there is the sense that if one is "doing good" socially, perhaps it's not so necessary to "do well" financially. Hence compensation is not at the appropriate professional level, a constant problem. Some mantras actually support this situation, among them, "You don't get rich in social work" and "Work for the truly needy, not the worried well."

Remedies

Remedies require structural and cultural change. Each agency has to live within its means, a consideration that requires it take on no more than it can afford while providing appropriate compensation (and adequate infrastructure). There also need to be counternarratives that legitimate reasonable, guilt-free compensation. Leaders in the community benefit sector need to model self-care, vacation time, appropriate compensation, and so on.

Problem: Expectations Are a Cut Above

Finally, there is the pressure of social expectations. Community benefit organizations may create a stress of their own, placing higher expectations on organization staff, relating to the service purpose of their mission. These higher expectations are problematic in their own right. In addition, they may add even more problems because their stakeholders tend to think of nonprofits and their staff as "more authentic" than corporate managers and less vulnerable to the range of human venalities available. It is likely that—whether implicitly or explicitly—managers and leaders have this view of themselves.

Remedies

Managers need to recognize that they (and all of us) are people, and none of us are exempt from the problems and temptations that beset all people everywhere. For personal peace of mind, the manager needs to recognize that he or she can do only so much to combat wicked problems and that it is okay to have a family and personal life outside of work. Indeed, performance in all areas will be better if managers attend to needs in each sector and do not ignore any sector. Understanding oneself as fallible permits greater understanding of others as fallible as well.

Managerially, you must be alert to staff and personal behavior, noticing signs that problems of integrity might be developing. Indicators include lying or omitting information, expense account padding, stealing office supplies, inappropriate use of the Internet at work, and so on. All of these (perhaps small) problems indicate the presence or development of larger issues. Early and *direct* confrontation is vital here. As the ad has it for parents and teenagers, urging parents to confront adolescents at the first sign of a substance issue, "Action: The Anti-Drug."

CONCLUSION

Much needs to be done to improve the executive and governance cadres of social work agencies. Our road is long and arduous. We have a lot of baggage, baggage that we have been taught to carry. But in this, as in all things, we have choice. We can choose to hem and haw, to propose SOSO (same old same old), to claim lack of resources, lack of appreciation, lack of support and a bad back, or we can strive to be, as the U.S. Army recruiting tagline has it, "Be All That You Can Be." Our clients and communities deserve no less.

REFLECTION

- Identify the industry, sector, and size of your community benefit organization. Of these factors, which most affects how you operate, what are your strengths, and where do you encounter limitations?
- Of the problems common to community benefit organizations discussed here, which do you most frequently grapple with? Why? How are you and your organization remedying and/or ameliorating the problem?
- Describe the function of the board of directors/trustees in your organization.

FURTHER READING

Carver, J. (2006). *Boards that make a difference*. San Francisco, CA: Jossey-Bass.

Stone Motes, P., & McCartt Hess, P. (2007). *Collaborating with community-based organizations through consultation and technical assistance*. New York, NY: Columbia University Press.

PART 3

The People Picture

Five Kinds of People and How to Manage Them

Now that we have a sense of managerial work and formal organizations, the setting in which much managerial work is undertaken, let's begin to unpack the specific competencies that will help you do it well. Managers have two general foci for their work: people and products. They are of course interrelated, but it will help us to address them separately. Two emphases are listed in Table P3.1. On the left are the people a manager must manage and lead: your managerial self, subordinates, peers, bosses, and your external network. Chapters 7 through 9 take these in turn. We examine columns 3 to 5 of Table P3.1 in part 4.

Table P3.1. Supervisory/Managerial Focus

Supervisory/Managerial People Focus		Supervisory/Managerial Product Focus		
Management Target	*Managing*	*Tasks*	*Projects*	*Systems/ Mission*
Yourself (and family)	In (within)	X	X	X
Your subordinates (direct reports)	Down	X	X	X
Your peers	Across		X	X
Your bosses	Up			X
Your external network	Out			X

7

Managing Yourself

INTRODUCTION

When we think of management and leadership, it is almost axiomatic that we look outward. Somehow managing is managing *others*. And, indeed, much management is management of others. However, that view circumvents the core of managerial centeredness: your own self. If you cannot manage yourself, then it is really not possible to manage much else.

Obviously this topic is the subject of volumes. Here, I highlight some of the most critical elements, some of which are frequently overlooked: stress and stress management and leadership, time management and leadership, issues of mental and physical health, temperament and emotional intelligence, and executive coaching. Part of managing yourself is managing (or managing with) your family. Because this topic is so important, I am including it here as well.

SOURCES OF STRESS AND STRAIN

Absence of stress—pressure to perform—is not good. We all need appropriate levels of stress to achieve current goals and develop toward future goals. Strain—stress in inappropriate amounts—injures us. What are the sources of stress/strain? Whetten and Cameron (2015) suggest:

- Anticipatory stress: Worry about what is to come
- Encounter stress: Specific difficult people
- Time stress: Never enough time
- Situational stress: Situations, such as public speaking, that upset us

Keeping this list in mind, some of the ideas in this chapter will certainly help.

APPROACHES TO STRESS MANAGEMENT AND STRAIN REDUCTION

A number of the approaches discussed here are interrelated and fall under the general headings of wellness and mindfulness.

Maintain Physical and Mental Energy

A healthy person needs energy to deal effectively with stress, no matter its source. As you lose energy, you run out of *cope,* my term for capacity to "deal" on any given day. Fatigue can limit your supply of cope, while rest and success can increase it. According to The Energy Project (n.d.), human beings require four sources of energy to operate at their best: physical, emotional, mental, and spiritual. All are necessary, but none is sufficient by itself. Low energy activates the "four horses "of low constrained contribution: fatigue, fear, distraction, and disengagement.

FATIGUE

Only 56% of employees feel physically energized at work.

Organizations are becoming more aware of the high cost of fatigue on employee focus, creativity, and performance.

FEAR

Fifty-eight percent of CEOs are concerned about lack of trust as a threat to the growth and success of their organizations.

Fear prompts people to narrowly focus on defending their value at the expense of creating value for their organizations.

DISTRACTION

Nearly 50% of employees find their meetings unfocused and inefficient.

Absorbed focus is more difficult than ever. Distraction undermines performance and creative thinking.

DISENGAGEMENT

Only 34% of employees feel a strong connection to their company's mission.

The result is low energy, inattention to detail and quality, lack of commitment, and high turnover.

Develop Resilience

Resilience is a bounce-back capacity that has physical as well as emotional components. It is part of what emotional intelligence literature calls *optimism,* the ability to press on in spite of setbacks. Resilience also emerges when you are able to contextualize experience, to cultivate the sense that you are connected to a force larger than yourself. This sense of connection is vital, for example, in every physical health assay.

Learn Temporary Coping Mechanisms

We all need "quick copers," my term for go-to practices that help us to refocus, recharge, and reenergize during sustained stressful experiences that are part and parcel of managerial work in formal organizations. These should be adaptive, or beneficial to overall well-being, rather than maladaptive, or damaging. Some practice centering prayer, or count to 10, or listen to music, or practice mindful breathing, or read a book. Automating these practices means that you quickly turn to them when you begin to reach your "wall" and are able to avoid making these situations worse or wearing yourself down.

It is particularly important to access temporary coping mechanisms when you are in a situation where the source, duration, or intensity of stress is likely to force you to your wall. Why? Intense stress robs us of our available repertoire of interactional styles. Interactional styles, or behavioral styles, are our available repertoire, much as our closet has an array of available ensembles. Some closets are full; others more sparse. Stress, ill health, and other variables can "clean our closet" so to speak. Under stress, we tend to revert to our default style, the one most native to us (see discussion on temperament later in this chapter) and that we are most comfortable with, *regardless of how (in)effective it is in the situation.* During periods of intense stress, we tend to seek out anything available that helps us feel comfortable, normal, or more in control, and we shift into our automatic or default relational setting. (By way of analogy, we also have default geographic settings. Have you ever, shortly after a move, "accidentally" driven to your former home?)

Manage and Lead Your Time

Time is the ultimate nonrenewable resource, the one thing we cannot get any more of. Stewarding this resource—commonly referred to as time management and leadership—falls into two major tasks: prioritization and schedule control.

Prioritization means understanding your ideal time distribution and the actual time distribution you have achieved (or defaulted to). The Index of Difference (see Table 7.1) can help you understand your current situation. In Table 7.1, I make some assumptions. One is that five areas of life, listed in column 1, are important. I also assume an ideal distribution selected by an ideal individual. In column 2, I assume that this person's real distribution was heavily work oriented, allowing little time for anything else. In column 3, I show the absolute difference for each row (the absolute difference disregards sign). I then add the differences in column 3 and divide by 2. The resulting quotient, the Index of Difference, shows how far apart the ideal and real time distributions are.

Table 7.1. Index of Difference

Life	Ideal (%)	Real (%)	Ideal-Real (%)
Personal	25	5	20
Family	25	15	10
Work	25	75	50
Civic	20	5	15
Other/ Miscellaneous	5	0	5
Total	100	100	100% divided by 2 = 50% Index of Difference

Try completing an Index of Difference (see reflection at the end of this chapter). If yours is over 15%, you are probably allocating more time to one of the dimensions than you wish you were. Typically, for managers, this happens with work. Work acts like a vacuum, dragging people and their time into its vortex. Civic time is usually the first to go, followed by personal and family time. Managers are often thrilled about the money they are making, not realizing they are working two jobs at the same workplace! Realizing that your schedule is disordered is the first step toward mastering it. Organizations are adept at getting people to work free or cheap; it is one of the ways they make money or break even. If you choose to contribute, fine. If you do not, then set boundaries and enforce limits. It is good to remember that work will absorb all the time you have to give it, and more. Be sure that you are wittingly and voluntarily allocating your time to it. This is one of the hardest lessons to learn and is a crucial part of self-management. It has always been difficult, but its difficulty has increased by an order of magnitude in our contemporary 24/7 "on-demand" work environment. Community benefit organizations have special problems here, as service demands increase and support for those with social needs becomes a less popular funding goal. The sum of these changes frequently leads to unrecognized social exploitation of these organizations. And managers, not always thinking clearly, coerce their employees to overwork.

Now that you have identified how you would like to prioritize and invest your time, develop means through which to actualize, implement, or execute the strategy. To start, you can use the Index of Difference within sectors (say job, family, and/or personal) to prioritize time within sectors—seeing if, and to what degree, they are important.

Locate and use a planning/calendaring system. Any system will do, as long as you use it. The Franklin system makes a special attempt to integrate strategic and tactical elements, with spaces to connect values to day-to-day activities. Managing and leading time is very much like managing and leading other aspects of yourself—health, wellness, and so on. It must be integrated into your day-to-day work. It's a challenge, perhaps the first challenge a manager faces, but if you do not control your schedule, it will control you, and your Index of Difference will zoom out of sight.

CULTIVATE HEALTH AND WELLNESS

It may seem odd that managers working in the community benefit sector should be reminded about the importance of mental and physical health. But humans are most likely to ignore those things they are good at when it comes to themselves. Health is often thought of as freedom from illness or injury. But that is too narrow; it also includes wellness, or the positive sense of being as well. And it is not only individuals who count but organizations as well. In fact, if it were up to me, I would change the Centers for Disease Control and Prevention to the Center for Health Promotion.

CULTIVATE MENTAL AND PHYSICAL HEALTH

We all know how important it is to steward our physical health. When asked if we do, we often reply, "Well, I'm trying." Unfortunately, effort does not always equal achievement. Work can quickly subsume time dedicated to the other areas of life that we value. If end-of-the-month reconciliations are due, or a grant performance evaluation is imminent, or a proposal is due, nothing is easier than skipping the gym, ordering takeout, going to bed late—you get the picture. Not only does this cycle impact your mental health, but it erodes physical health as well. Of course, preventative information is readily available, but it is so prevalent that it is sometimes difficult to discern what is meaningful and what is conjecture. Moreover, mental and physical health are often intertwined, and it's difficult to distinguish between effects on one or the other. I offer a few perennial suggestions next.

CULTIVATING MENTAL AND PHYSICAL HEALTH

1. Cultivate self-awareness.
   Make space to honestly assess what you're experiencing. Be truthful about strengths and deficits. Elicit your assumptions: Ask what, then ask why. Periodically challenge these assumptions: Are they grounded in reality or fiction?
2. Take time to reflect.
   Make space, away from electronics, to reflect on the events of the day, your responses to them, and what your responses tell you about your well-being.

3. Identify your professional limits.
   Articulate to yourself what you can and cannot tolerate on the job (conditions, treatment, stress, responsibility, hostility, meaning and purpose, compensation). Revisit and revise these in advance of changing circumstances.

4. Don't numb your feelings.
   Avoid handling everyday stressors and uniquely difficult situations with chemicals, food, or unhealthy relational patterns. If you notice yourself depending on these, ask for help.

5. Make friends with change and frustration.
   Change and frustration are part and parcel of the professional experience. Identify those things that help you weather both without hurting yourself or others. Exercise? Meditation? Mind-body work? Commitment to a higher cause?

6. Know the darker side of your nature and contain it.
   Each of us has a destructive, revenge-seeking side. Each of us also has the propensity to misuse power for personal reasons. Be alert to these and ensure that your professional and personal circumstances have checks and balances in place.

7. Avoid comparison, but embrace a growth mindset.
   This is nearly impossible in a meme-and-soundbite culture. To the best of your ability, use best practices and prior performance as benchmarks, but avoid interpersonal comparisons. Welcome adversity and failure as pathways to growth, and remind yourself often that growth is the goal.

8. Choose role models and friends carefully.
   Be wise in the selection of companions. You become like the people you emulate and the people with whom you surround yourself.

9. Prepare for possible loneliness.
   As you move up in your organization, colleagues tend to move away. Accept this, but be vigilant against isolation. If you find yourself without a community, seek out a coach/mentor and take steps to build a new community.

10. Trust others, but don't be a doormat.
    If you do not trust, you will spend all your time and energy checking the work of others. Some will not deserve your trust, and you will have to take the heat for their errors. Move on. Do not trust more than once. (Unlike baseball, one strike is enough.)

11. Move.
    "Sitting is the new smoking." If you are working in a sedentary position, make regular time throughout the day to stand, stretch, walk, or go outside. Incorporate strength training and cardio into your weekly routine. Gym and yoga? Sure. But if you're short on time, consider only taking the stairs, commuting via bike or by foot, adding light weights to your yard or housework tasks, or another creative option.

12. Sleep sufficiently, and well.

Most of us fail to secure enough sleep; we should be aiming for no fewer than six hours, and more if possible. We should also work to protect our sleep architecture and hygiene—avoiding screen time and excessive stimuli prior to turning in; steering ourselves away from alcohol, caffeine, consistent use of over-the-counter sleep aids; and ensuring a dark, quiet, distraction-free environment in which to sleep.

13. Eat well.

Nutrition is highly bioindividual. The definition of "eating well" depends on your genetic profile, food sensitivities, environment, age, activity level, job type, stress level, sleep profile, and other factors. Know yourself; know what works for you; and build a plan that is manageable. If you aren't sure what works best, don't rely on the latest cool thing; find a nutritionist or a wellness coach whom you trust.

13. Decompress.

Identify mindfulness-based stress-reduction techniques that resonate with you and practice them routinely. Untether and power down every day and for an extended period each weekend. Identify nature and social experiences that resonate with you (forest bathing? potluck with friends?) and schedule these.

14. Maintain relationships with medical professionals and attend to preventative care.

Much like regular oil changes and routine maintenance are necessary for keeping your vehicle in optimal working order, annual physicals, dental check-ups, physical therapy assessments, and therapist and psychiatrist check-ins are key to caring for your mental and physical health and heading off problems before they arise, or before they burgeon out of control.

It's not hard to connect the dots between chronic neglect of mental and physical health and subpar performance, impaired decision-making, and disruptions in the office and at home. If you're not operating well, physically, mentally, or both, your capacity to lead and manage is impaired. Perhaps no one will notice at first. But left unaddressed, those stresses will result in relational tone deafness, lack of personal "cope," reduced staff morale and performance, and potential flame-out. Take care of yourself.

Temperament

I like to think of temperament as your own preferred and usual behavioral personality (though not your only one). Understanding temperament—yours and others'—is important because it helps you to understand yourself, your likely response to circumstances and interactions, and the strengths and weaknesses inherent in your temperament. Over the second half of the 20th century, a range of sophisticated assessments has been developed and implemented. Among the most widely used are the Myers-Briggs Type Indicator (MBTI), Strengths Finder, Emotional Quotient, Enneagram, and DiSC. (The latter one focuses on communication styles.)

All assessments have strengths and weaknesses. Take time to find one that you like, familiarize yourself with it, and think about it. Process it with others. The process of reflection and review is perhaps as valuable as the method employed in any specific assessment. Whatever name you give it, each of us has a default style of interacting. When someone asks, "What is John Tropman like?" the answer will largely reflect my default style, my core. While assays may not comprehensively synthesize our entire core, they do shed light on it, helping us to know ourselves—and, as managers and leaders, that is vital to our efficiency and effectiveness in the organization and in other areas of our lives.

You can make two kinds of errors regarding temperament assays. One is to ignore them completely. If you take that path, you lose the ability to learn from reflection and to glean any specific information about your "core." The other error is to become too involved with any specific selfportrait provided by one assay. Remember, they reflect you, rather than define you. Therefore "use it, don't refuse or abuse it."

THE MYERS-BRIGGS

The Myers-Briggs is the most widespread and applied assay around. It has its critics, of course, but it also has construct validity, judging from its ubiquity and application over time. According to Myers-Briggs thinking, each of us has one dominant set of characteristics that defines our "type." However, some of us are really strong with one or more dimensions. Dominant characteristics require the most attention, because they are most noticeable, and others tend to characterize them as personality.

It is important to understand that our approach to daily life is structured, rather than random, and has patterning and themes, rather than arbitrariness. A snapshot of our temperaments helps us relate to ourselves and others relate to us, but it can also become rigid and repetitive. Once you have a sense of your temperament, you can be more operationally aware of when its display is appropriate. Further, you can experiment with other temperaments and styles. Myers-Briggs analyses explicitly discuss the "Shadow Side," the temperament that is exactly the opposite from you. Take some time to explore the shadow side and broaden your repertoire.

THE STRENGTHS FINDER

The Strengths Finder was developed from the work of the Gallup Organization. It has four "leadership domains" and 34 themes, listed next. The four domains are the overall "buckets" into which the Gallup Organization places its themes. Generally they address our ability to:

- Get things done
- Get others on board
- Connect with others
- Think ahead.

Four Domains of Leadership Strength

Executing:
Team members who have a dominant strength in the executing domain are those you turn to time and again to implement a solution. These are the people who will work tirelessly to get something done. They consistently transform ideas into reality within the organizations they lead.

Influencing:
People who are innately good at influencing are always selling the team's ideas inside and outside the organization. When you need someone to take charge, speak up, and make sure your group is heard, look to someone with the strength to influence.

Relationship Building:
Relationship builders are the glue that holds a team together. Strengths associated with bringing people together — whether it is by keeping distractions at bay or keeping the collective energy high — transform a group of individuals into a team capable of carrying out complex projects and goals.

Strategic Thinking:
Those who are able to keep people focused on "what they could be" are constantly pulling a team and its members into the future. They continually absorb and analyze information and help the team make better decisions.

Each domain has several themes from within the overall 34 that "cluster" and give it operational power. These themes are the muscle of the domain; they give it strength.

Executing Themes:
These nine themes are the hardest working of the bunch. They tend to get things done, with speed, precision, and accuracy. They put in the hard work now, so that when it's time to move, they are ready. Putting ideas into action is the strength of this domain. They are:

Achiever; Arranger; Belief; Consistency; Deliberative; Discipline; Focus; Responsibility; Restorative

Influencing Themes:
These eight themes enable individuals or groups to sell the big ideas. They are able to take charge, speak up, and be heard. They are extremely helpful when you need to reach a broader audience or meet a bigger goal. This can happen both internally or externally. They tend to influence forward. They are:

Activator; Command; Communication; Competition; Maximizer; Self-Assurance; Significance; Woo (Wooing Others Over)

Relationship Building Themes:
While certainly not the only themes that deal with people (because they're all about people), these nine themes have an innate ability to take the human component into the equation. They look at how individuals fit into the bigger picture and can create pathways for them to thrive. They make strong relational connections that bind a group together around a cause, idea, or each other. They are:

Adaptability; Developer; Connectedness; Empathy; Harmony; Includer; Individualization; Positivity; Relator

Strategic Thinking Themes:
When a plan needs to be made, or a new idea created for solving a problem, these eight themes can help accomplish that. Whether it's thinking into a current problem or dreaming about how to overcome tomorrow's, the strategic thinking themes can take a thought or idea and look for the best way to move forward on it. These are:

Analytical; Context; Futuristic; Ideation; Input; Intellection; Learner; Strategic.

What is the relationship between the Myers-Briggs and Strengths Finder approaches? I consider MBTI categories dispositions, and Gallup categories skills. For example, in the Myers-Briggs assessment, I am an ENTJ (Extraverted, iNtuitive, Thinking, Judging). An occupational area frequently associated with this "type" is field marshal. Field marshals oversee the entire field of battle and are the large-scale strategists. A maestro also might be a good term as well. My top five themes (strengths) are as follows, in order:

- Futuristic: Executing Domain
- Activator: Influencing Domain
- Ideation: Strategic Domain
- Strategic: Strategic Domain
- Achiever: Executing Domain

I think the package describes me very well. However, I also have to look at my "shadow side" as well as the missing relationship domains to be sure I am not overusing my natural skills.

EMOTIONAL INTELLIGENCE
I mentioned emotional intelligence and the emotion quotient (EQ) earlier when we were talking about feelings in the workplace. Failure to recognize and manage our own feelings is one of the important causes of managerial failure. Its stunning rise to wide application in managerial circles is proof that it has certainly uncovered an area of importance, even if you do not always agree with its specific points.

Emotional intelligence work began with Edward Thorndike in the 1930s. Kendra Cherry (2017) offers a good summary. In particular she mentions the work of Howard Gardner and Daniel Goleman. Here are the most common dimensions of EQ (numerous other assays are publicly available):

- *Self-Awareness*
  Knowing what you feel
- *Management/Leadership of Feelings*
  Controlling impulses
  Soothing your anxiety
  Having appropriate anger
- *Motivation*
  Zeal, persistence, and optimism in the face of setbacks
- *Empathy*
  Reading and responding to unspoken feelings (someone crying in your office does not count)
- *Social Skills*
  Handling emotional reactions in others
  Interacting smoothly
  Managing relationships effectively

These may seem obvious to those serving in community benefit organizations. However, we are often not better than others when it comes to understanding ourselves. Therefore, as with temperament, EQ is a useful framework within which to understand important aspects of ourselves.

One advantage to EQ is that it has a range of assessment tools; in fact measuring EQ has become something of a cottage industry. As with the MBTI, use EQ assays to gain insight, rather than make a determination, about yourself.

What is the case for investing your time and energy in one more tool, one more task? Aren't there enough demands on your energy and plenty of apps to help you keep track of them all? Well, sure. But you know that management is, in both task and relationship focus, fast-paced and intense. It requires harmonizing competing priorities and often-clashing personalities to achieve organizational work. It's hard to harmonize, let alone understand, without a sketch of who you are and, ideally, who your coworkers are. You also know that, in the effort to achieve work, feelings will arise—your own and others'. You need to be able to recognize, identify, channel, and sometimes even resolve them. This is an iterative responsibility much more easily achieved if you understand your own temperament. The implications of ignoring temperament include alienation from your own emotions, "tone-deafness" in interpersonal situations, and disconnection from the informal organizational structure, which will ultimately undermine your authority and make it difficult to motivate and lead, rather than force.

EXECUTIVE COACHING

Managing yourself is difficult to begin with, and even more difficult to do alone. Don't hesitate to secure a well-trained professional executive coach. Note that a coach is distinct from a mentor. A mentor is a friend or colleague who is willing and happy to help—up to an often ill-defined point. A coach may perform some mentor-like functions but is a consultant whom you pay to help you gain perspective and grow professionally. Just as all competent therapists have a didactic therapist who reviews and talks through cases with them, executive coaches help you to grow beyond your current circumstances. It is important to find someone to whom you can talk on a regular basis and who knows both managerial issues and your sector. It is in investment in your future. Do not hesitate to make it. Your coach is one of the array of professionals you have available to help you with your life (lawyer, plumber, etc.). In much of the community benefit sector, programs for and support of managerial development are extremely thin. Moreover, some issues—such as career development and job searches—are best discussed in a relationship completely separate from your organization. You do not have to use a coach on a regular basis. After an initial assessment, coaching should be manager-activated. Sometime you will need to talk with the coach a few times a week, then not for many months. It depends on what is going on with you and your work. Informal coaching does not replace the expertise of a seasoned, well-trained professional executive coach. However, it can be relatively simple to form a meet-up or reading group of local professionals who are roughly your contemporaries. It can be a women's reading group (especially important as women have historically had less support in managerial roles than men), all men, mixed, or whatever. As Sheryl Sandberg (2014) says, "When I ask men if they have been called bossy just a few hands go up; when I ask women, every hand goes up!" It is good to have a pretext for getting together, since setting up a group, especially among males, can imply that we are in less than complete control and want to discuss our "issues." This may spook potential participants—hence the indirect method works better than the direct one.

MANAGING (WITH) YOUR FAMILY

This topic is complex, shifting, and worthy of volumes. Not only is it is heavily gendered, but it combines all domains of management and leadership—self, peer, subordinate, boss; and internal and external networks. Moreover, it is a complex blend of managerial demands and activities. The now-cliché concept of work–life balance is a vital component of family management: We work for ourselves but also for our families. If success at work means that your family never sees you, chances are, your Index of Difference (see Table 7.1) is too high. James Thurber's (1945) story about the drinking bear illustrates this point. He would drink then crash around breaking furniture and making a mess. He went into ABA (Alcoholic Bears Anonymous), got a personal trainer, became extremely fit, and would illustrate this by crashing around, breaking furniture, and making a mess. The moral of the story is, "You may as well fall flat on your face as lean too far over backward!"

Cooperative management is another aspect of family management. In organizing your family culture, remember the success/sacrifice equation: Everyone's success depends to some extent on others' sacrifices, whether or not they are recognized. Make explicit and examine those sacrifices. Ensure that everyone feels they're worthwhile. If they do not, then make space for adjustment and alteration of goals and trajectories.

What does this look like in contemporary family life? Spouses and partners of managers are likely to be professional as well; there are frequently two careers to manage, not one. Not only do you need to explore strategic issues like family culture, goals, and trajectories, but it's also vital to move to the operational level and hammer out issues of sequencing, primacy, and timing, preferably in advance. Of course, the many complex factors informing and shaping operational-level issues can make such conversations sensitive and difficult.

This sensitivity and difficulty can be compounded when managers forget to use their hard-earned managerial skills in the family setting.[1] Many family and career issues need to be discussed in, well, meetings. But having a family meeting seems odd, even though that is exactly how managers address an issue in a formal organizational setting—not that meetings go well there, either (see chapter 13). If possible, work at actually having a family meeting with your spouse or partner (and older children too) to consider family values and goals and how those form the foundation for a longer-range family strategic plan. It will help you all value one another and your hopes, dreams, and aims. But it will help you to be flexible too, as circumstances on the ground evolve and change.

A third component of family management involves the unique role of women who manage in formal organizations and have significant family management responsibilities as well. If there are children in the family, women usually have, according to Hochschild and Machung (1989), a second job before they leave for, and when they get home from, formal employment. For many women, work is a relaxation, a place filled with respect, deference, appreciation, and little pee and pooh. Women managers often feel guilty when at work and when not at work. They especially need the support and affirmation from other working moms.

Families have a complex set of needs and requirements. As organizations (to take that narrow view for a moment), they present a special challenge because they involve deep levels of commitment, incorporate the emotions that both bind and separate members, and encompass complicated and often unacknowledged role expectations (of self, partner, children, and other relatives). Given these many organizational challenges, it is astonishing—and to be celebrated— that they succeed as well as they do.

CONCLUSION

In this chapter we have made explicit what we all, at some level, intuit: We are our own first direct reports. In contemporary settings, management and leadership are almost always conceptualized as other-directed and external. However, the

---

1. It is for this reason I included a chapter on the "family meeting" in *Meetings: How to Make Them Work for You* (2002).

core of management is managing your own self, and we touched on a few important components of self-management that are inherent in the managerial and leadership experience: stress, time, health, temperament, emotional intelligence, external support, and family.

REFLECTION

- What areas of stress do you experience? Why?
  - Anticipatory stress: Worry about what is to come
  - Encounter stress: Specific difficult people
  - Time stress: Never enough time
  - Situational stress: Situations, like public speaking, that upset us
- How is your Index of Difference?

Table 7.2 shows a sample index of difference that you can use or copy for your own use. Give it a try! Ask your partner or spouse to fill out one as well and compare: They can do it for you, or you can do two sets—one reflecting the ideal and one reflecting reality.

- What are your go-to tools for short-term stress reduction? If you don't have an explicit toolkit, what could you easily incorporate and automate?
- What are your long-term strategies for personal growth? How do these align with your temperament and/or your EQ?
- How is your EQ? Give a top-of-mind response to the following questions (0 = never, 5 = always). If your score is under 45, consider seeking out opportunities to grow in this area.
  1. I am aware of even subtle feelings as I have them.
  2. I find myself using my feelings to help make big decisions.
  3. When I am angry, I blow my top or fume in silence.
  4. Bad moods overwhelm me, and it takes a long time to regain equilibrium.

Table 7.2. Blank Index of Difference

Life	Ideal	Real	Ideal-Real
Personal			
Family			
Work			
Civic			
Other/ Miscellaneous			
Total	100%	100%	Index of Difference

5. I can delay gratification in pursuit of my goals instead of getting carried away by impulse.

6. When I am anxious about a challenge, I can't prepare well.

7. Instead of giving up in the face of setbacks, I stay hopeful.

8. People don't have to tell me what they feel; I can sense it.

9. My keen sense of others' feelings gives me compassion for their plight.

10. I have trouble handling conflict and emotional upset.

11. I can sense the pulse of a group and unspoken feelings.

12. I can soothe my distressing feelings so they don't keep me from doing what I have to do.

13. I can express myself in a constructive, team-building way, even in a difficult circumstance

14. Other people aren't afraid to tell me the truth, even if it's uncomfortable.

15. I can separate my feelings about a task from completing the task itself.

FURTHER READING

Blanchard, K. (1999). *The one-minute manager balances work and life.* New York, NY: William Morrow.

Blanchard, K. (2017). *Self-leadership and the one-minute manager.* New York, NY: William Morrow.

Bradford, D., & Cohen, A. (1997). *Managing for excellence.* Hoboken, NJ: Wiley.

CliftonStrengths Assessment. (n.d.). www.gallupstrengthscenter.com

Gebelein, S., et al. (2010). *The successful managers handbook: Develop yourself, coach others* (8th ed.). Los Angeles, CA: Korn Ferry Leadership Consulting.

Lombardo, M., & Barnfield, H. (2014). *FYI: For your improvement—Competencies development guide* (6th ed.). Minneapolis, MN: Korn Ferry.

Network for Social Work Management, Human Services Management Competencies. (n.d.). www.socialworkmanager.org

Schwartz, T., & McCarthy, C. (2007, October). Manage your energy, not your time. *Harvard Business Review.* https://hbr.org/2007/10/manage-your-energy-not-your-time

Weiss, L. (2018). *How we work.* New York, NY: HarperWave.

8

Managing Subordinates

Building Staff Performance

INTRODUCTION

The aim of managing subordinates is building staff performance. Setting goals; implementing a system for informing, coaching, and evaluating; and learning to allocate energy among types of staff will help you become both effective and efficient. Rather than giving you a comprehensive overview of personnel management from onboarding to off-ramping employees, step by infinitesimal step, let's assume you're already in position and explore how, *in medias res*, you can begin to build staff performance. To do this we'll explore two aspects of staff performance: project work and overall performance.

STRUCTURING THE MANAGERIAL ARCHITECTURE

In building staff performance, whatever the skill package, start with goals—things you want your staff to strive *toward*, not failures you want them to avoid. While the content of goals will depend upon the situation, using a framework to articulate them will help you and your staff start from a place of clarity and understanding. Consider frameworks like SMART and SUCCESS, simple mnemonic devices to assist in touching important bases in goal setting.

SMART goals are:
  Specific (simple, sensible, significant)
  Measurable (meaningful, motivating)
  Achievable (agreed, attainable)
  Relevant (reasonable, realistic and resourced, results-based)
  Time bound (time-based, time-limited, time/cost limited, timely, time-sensitive)

SUCCESS goals are:

Simple
Understandable
Competence driven
Communicated clearly
Equitable
Sustain enthusiasm
Share vision

If your goals do not meet those criteria, reconceptualize them so that they do. As a manager, it's not advisable to ask your staff, "What kind of work do you want to do?" It's much better to place them in the context of the organization. For example, "Our team is charged with contributing X to the Y initiative. I'd like you to play Z part in that. Within this framework, what would an outstanding performance look like? How can we measure or quantify it?"

PROJECT ASSESSMENT

Managers and leaders juggle a host of competing priorities, so they need a system to help them stay in touch with staff and staff performance. The first step is meeting with staff to set goals. The second is to agree on checking in or monitoring. What will it look like? How often will it happen? The frequency varies, as some staff require more and others less. But you work toward occasional check-ins, since your time is finite. Third, establish milestones, significant outputs necessary to achieving an outcome. Assessment takes the pulse of project progress. It asks where you are with respect to project goals, schedule, budget, and progress toward them. Are you on time, ahead of time, behind? Knowing that, you can take appropriate remedial steps; reschedule; or remain on a steady course. Assessment is usually done in thirds or quarters, over however long the time period for the project. If there is a 90-day project, then every month might work. This occurs so that there can be "midcourse corrections," if any are needed.

At the conclusion of the project, managers conduct an appraisal and develop what, in military circles, is called the "after-action report." While the appraisal reviews records and objective measures of the project, it also includes an experiential review of the project. Much like a realtor will use his or her personal judgement of comparable sales, curb appeal, interior improvements, neighborhood strength, and market solidity when pricing a house, a manager assessing a project will use personal judgement, insight, and experience to review the project. This is the indispensable art that goes along with the science of project management. The conclusion of that report is a "lessons learned" section. These lessons are part of the harvesting process through which organizational learning occurs.

PERFORMANCE APPRAISAL

Performance appraisals consider a staff member's total performance for a year, or any defined period of time. This process is distinct from, but related to, project assessment, which is a part of the overall performance appraisal. It is important to give periodic but frequent feedback regarding project performance. This process is called the performance audit. Performance appraisals often go awry so I am adding a longer discussion of their elements here.

TAKING A BROADER VIEW

As we look over the range of staff performance, it is important to consider the distribution of staff quality. It will, of course, vary by organization sector, size, and function, but some general guidelines are broadly applicable. First is the staff version of the modified 80/20 rule, commonly formulated as 80% of your results come from 20% of your workers. That seems a bit extreme. Here's a more reasonable version:

- 20% of your workers are excellent.
- 60% are satisfactory.
- 20% are unsatisfactory or subpar.

I have found that there is a lot of agreement among working managers that these proportions are generally accurate, though as I said, individual workplaces do differ.

The distribution of managerial energy along this continuum is standard as well. Lots of time is given to those at the bottom; minimal time is given to the middle (with more being allocated as staff get closer to the bottom) and very little to the top 20%. The presence of problematic staff is a double cost: The nonproductive drain your time and keep you from assisting the regularly productive and super productive. Generally, your time should be proportional to staff types. Spending much more than 20% of your time with the unsatisfactory or subpar workers is a problem.

A clearer analysis emerges when managers look at staff performance as made up of success and failures (Table 8.1), consider staff positions on the success/failure grid, and allocate their time appropriately. Keep in mind that the most problematic, really, are the shooting-star workers. They are problematic because they are good *and* bad. Managers and leaders are often likely to overlook the bad until it becomes really bad, and staff often overlook their own problems as well, focusing on the good they also do. This can make for a deadly combination, because the cost of the pain and dissension and cultural collapse produced by the behavior of the talented employee is vastly greater than the gains he or she produces.

In the grid, managers should employ "differential use of self" not only in terms of time but in directing work with these individuals. (Differential use of self means

Table 8.1. Success/Failure Grid

		THINGS GONE RIGHT		
		Few	Some	Many
THINGS GONE WRONG	Few	1. So-So Worker 10%	2. Satisfactory Worker 10%	3. Excellent Worker 20%
	Some	4. Problem Worker 10%	5. Satisfactory Worker 10%	6. Good Worker 20%
	Many	7. Problem Worker 10%	8. So-So Worker 5%	9. Shooting Star Worker 10%

Source: Tropman, 2006; no permission/credit required.

tailoring, somewhat, your interaction to the needs and styles of "the other" even if that is not your preference. While it is often used by therapeutic professionals, it has much day-to-day application as well.) For staff in cells 4 and 7 (problem workers), managers should move toward outplacement. They are not doing much right and they are doing many things wrong. It is time to move on. Those in cells 1 and 8 (so-so workers) need specific, tight, corrective action plans. If correction does not follow, move toward outplacement. Cells 2, 5, and 6 (satisfactory and good staff) need support and development.

Some community benefit organization managers whom I interviewed, especially those in human services, feel that having "outplacement" agendas for 35% of staff is draconian (cells 1 + 4 + 7 + 8). Of course, that would be true if you used some kind of forced ranking system. But outplacement is not the initial option and, if you appraise your work teams honestly, you should not be tolerating people in those cells for very long. Not only do they not do the job (problem 1), and steal your time (problem 2), but they also poison the workplace through bad examples and undermine the work you are doing with others (problem 3). Finally, they make you look bad because you are not taking action (problem 4). Managers do try to be helpful. But organizations seldom exist solely to support staff; they exist to supply a product or service that benefits the community. You are paying staff to assist in that function. As the cliché has it, "if they are not part of the solution, they are part of the problem."

I saved cells 3 (excellent workers) and 9 (shooting-star workers) for last because they, rather than the others, represent your most serious problems and should be the focus of your efforts, even though the two groups represent two entirely different patterns of concern. The excellent staff in cell 3 hardly seem to be a problem. The problem is that we are inclined to ignore them, because things are going well and there is no reason to interfere. Some managers even rationalize *not* attending to them on the grounds that "if it ain't broke, don't fix it" and "leave well enough alone," and so on. These staff, like all humans, need support and appreciation. Their excellence no doubt involves going an extra mile. And remember excellent workers always have options, as other organizations would love to "poach" them from you. Disregarding them significantly increases your risk of losing them. They can, and will, leave.

Cell 9, shooting-star staff, are a different issue. These individuals do an outstanding job, like those in cell 3, but also mess up badly as well. In many ways these are the most difficult to deal with because it is hard to discuss their problems in the face of their achievement. And because they are good and bad, they use their good to blunt their bad. They tend, as do we all, to lionize achievements and minimize failures. Because their problems are the most likely to go unattended, undiscussed, and/or un-remedied, these problems have, and often realize, the potential to grow very large—involving not only the shooting-star worker but also the entire organization and its community (Tropman & Sheafer, 2004).

Managers need to emotionally and empirically prepare themselves for meeting with these individuals and doing it sooner rather than later. Also, while full acknowledgment of the positives needs to be made, it must be made clear that this meeting focuses upon the problem areas. A good way to do this is to email the individuals in question with a complimentary introduction, a list of the problematic areas, and a question for the respondent about how he or she intends to address these issues. Then the manager asks for a note before the meeting, so that the manager has a chance to review it. Tight structure is vital here.

These failures and mess-ups can (and often do) become flameouts and derailments that adversely affect the brand, reputation, and mission of the organization. To head off this danger, managers need to identify shooting-star workers and intervene before a problem escalates. Is there a proven formula for making this an "unawkward" conversation? Not really. But the following guidelines are broadly applicable:

1. Timing (regular performance assessment or special meeting)
2. Preparation (research, documentation, and human resources support, if needed)
3. Structure (two person, third party, recording; tone; focus)
4. Follow-through (support, benchmarks for improvement, next steps)

CONCLUSION

In this chapter, we considered what it means to build staff performance and how you can, to paraphrase Arthur Ashe, start where you are; use what you have; and do what you can to motivate, encourage, and hold your staff accountable for excellent performance. We also examined general varieties of performance and how to allocate your managerial energy among different types of employees.

REFLECTION

- What is your process for goal setting?
- Where are your staff in the cells?
- Do you need to take any action?
- How do you prepare for a potentially tense conversation? What additional skills for managing these conversations would be helpful to add to your repertoire?

FURTHER READING

Buckingham, M. (1999). *First break all the rules: What the world's greatest managers do differently.* New York, NY: Simon & Schuster.

Bustin, G. (2014). *Accountability: The key to driving a high-performance culture.* New York, NY: McGraw-Hill Education.

9

Managing Your Boss, Peers, and External Networks

INTRODUCTION

In addition to managing yourself and your staff (managing in), you also manage your peers (across), your boss (up), and out (your external network). It is to the last three topics that we turn now. They differ from managing yourself and your staff because you are working from the "second position." That is, you have responsibility but no authority. When you manage with authority, it's easier to feel uptight and anxious because you are fundamentally accountable for the performance and fit of yourself and your staff. If this accountability weighs heavily on you, if your staff aren't performing well (see chapter 8), or if your organizational culture is toxic (see chapters 4 and 5), you may default to the "Because I said so" approach or the "My way or the highway" option may be more to your liking.

On the other hand, when you manage your boss, peers, and external network, you have no authority to deploy the "Because I said so" approach or the "My way or the highway" option. You have to build relationships, connect to the target, and get the target to "want to do" what it should do anyway. Unfortunately, many managers don't pivot from the authority approach to the relationship approach when they attempt to manage in a no-authority setting. They may also invert themselves when they are interacting with their bosses, hence be essentially a "lion" to subordinates and a "lamb" with their bosses. None of these techniques works very well over time. Let's explore what does.

MANAGING YOUR BOSS

The boss is perceived as the most crucial individual in your network because generally the boss is the person who can fire you. If the boss does not fire you, he or she can make your life either miserable or great. Thus, establishing a good relationship with the boss is crucial. The way to approach this is to think of your boss as someone to be "managed," not in a sly way or a way that "spins" information to get what you want but one that treats the boss as an (internal) customer. While there is no accounting for the myriad "boss" personalities and organizational cultures, I offer some observations synthesized from years of research and coaching.

Rule 1: To Manage Your Boss Well, Manage Yourself Well

Remember, the boss wants you to help the boss. The boss does not want to spend an inordinate amount of time helping you. (Note that this does not apply to onboarding and training. Healthy organizations have a well-defined protocol for onboarding new employees and training them that extends far beyond handing you office keys and an employee handbook.) If your actions, or inactions, create traffic into the boss's office, or problems for the boss to solve, you have failed to implement Rule 1.

Rule 2: Start Where The Boss Is, Style Wise

Generally, you do this by understanding, first, the boss's preferred style. This is a broad term that encompasses all the ways the boss takes in and interacts with the world. Our bosses, like us, have temperaments. They have preferred ways to get energy, to get information, to make decisions, and to be open or closed. Some work "on the fly"; others like regular meetings of a more formal sort. Some like talking first and reading second; others like to read a proposal first and then talk about it. Your first approach is to give the boss information in the way the boss wants it. As Steven Covey (1990) says, "seek first to understand, then to be understood."

Rule 3: Show Commitment to the Organization

A successful organization reflects first on the boss. If you help the organization look good, you help the boss look good. (See Rules 1 and 8.) Representing the organization may involve doing a little extra work and then representing the organization and acting on behalf of it. (Be careful that you do not always step in to the "just a little extra" role.)

Rule 4: Carefully Select the Issues You Bring to the Boss

Depending on style, position in the organization, position of the organization in the community, and a host of other factors, the boss may be a high- or low-information manager (see Rule 1). Learn the sort of information and issues you should plan to communicate and those you should plan to resolve at your level. One criterion for resolving/escalating should be the issue's potential for visibility and exposure. (I call this *visiposure,* or visbility + exposure; communications people might call it branding, or coherence.) Your boss likes, and needs, to look competent, effective, and on top of things. If an issue has a high potential for being internally or externally public, your boss needs to know about it. When you bring issues to the boss, frame them in terms of results and outcomes, not just outputs. Your boss is accountable to the board, to funders, and to the public trust. None of these entities really cares how many meetings you took. They care about accomplishments. Thus, so does your boss.

There is one more point here: "appropriate self-promotion." Your boss has many peers, superiors, and direct and indirect reports. There is every possibility that he or she does not know as much as you might think about what you are actually doing. So you need to consider a personal marketing plan, so to speak, to increase your personal visiposure with the boss, This effort must be carefully timed and "every so often" so as not to be (or appear to be) grandstanding—a foible that will irritate your boss and your colleagues. But saying or showing nothing about your achievement or the value you contribute to the organization is not a good option either.

Rule 5: Exhibit Courage and Honesty, With Tact

We all do stupid things, bosses included. If you need to point out a problem, or disagree with the boss, do it diplomatically and privately, never in public. If you are "trapped" in a meeting where a boss says, "Everyone agrees, right?" You can say, "It certainly sounds good; let me just run over a few details and I will get back to you later today." The more the boss wants something, the less likely employees are to disagree, especially in public. (See chapter 14, discussion on decision quality.)

Rule 6: Get the Boss in Early

Get the boss in the loop early in any area where the boss has a known interest— whether a new initiative, a reformulated project, or a new phase of an ongoing priority—and, taking preferred communication styles into consideration, make a work plan with the boss. Get both positive and negative feedback on the plan and on your progress. You can use the Index of Difference (see chapter 7, Table 7.1) to rate the different emphases you and the boss may place on varied aspects of a project. This can be a real source of friction—and it often remains implicit, uni-dentified, and unexpressed and festers. Getting the boss in early is especially vital for issues in which the boss might have special interest or issues that might be po-litically sensitive or involve high-level stakeholders. As you work on such issues, be sure to give the boss ample credit.

Rule 7: Keep the Boss's Key Advisors Informed as Well

Find out—through observation or via the informal organizational structure—who the boss listens to (besides you). If the boss trusts them, you should show you also trust them by involving them in some way in your ideas and suggestions (but without imposing on them any additional responsibility), listening to them, and offering (if appropriate) your assistance. This builds your credibility. And, if the boss asks them to evaluate ideas you have, a positive word from the boss's trusted advisors cannot hurt.

Rule 8: Help the Boss Look Good

Bosses, like the rest of us, like—and need—to look good. This means giving the boss positive feedback and occasionally (though perhaps not as much as they deserve) negative feedback. To help the boss look good (i.e., competent, effective, far-sighted, and on top of all issues), make certain not to upstage him or her, even if you and/or your team are responsible for an organizational win. Remember, looking good in front of the boss is good, as long as it does not make your boss look bad.

Rule 9: "Manage" Toxic Bosses and Organizations

The rules here do not apply to bosses with special problems or toxicities. Among other problems, they may be mentally or physically ill, jaded and burnt out, green and in over their head, or just plain incompetent. Schwantes (2017) synthesizes research on the dangerous behaviors of such managers into eight general categories, including those who only look after themselves; steal the spotlight; are never wrong; don't have a specific strategic direction; need to control; bully; are missing in action; and are narcissists.

How to manage a toxic boss without compromising your physical and mental well-being is a book in its own right and, in my experience, a Sisyphean task. It is so much easier to change yourself than it is to hold out hope that the boss will change or that you will be able to hold up and be effective, let alone flourish, under the pressure and uncertainty that a difficult boss provokes. My first recommendation, if you have the option, is that you relocate. Even if you can't immediately make the change, at least begin to plan and prepare for it. As stressful as changing jobs can be, it is much less stressful than continuing to work under a dangerous manager. Of course, not everyone can or will change jobs, but those who have often ask me, "Why did I wait so long?"

And if you are stuck, and you find yourself needing to stay in an impaired-dignity situation for the long term, draw on the wealth of resources developed by others who've been there (see a few recommendations at the end of this chapter);

build a solid support network; and do your best to cultivate dignity at work and in other areas of life.

The other side of toxicity is when the workplace itself is toxic (which may, but does not have to, include a toxic boss). White (2015) developed a useful list of five danger signs:

1. Unhealthy communication patterns
2. Nonexistent or poorly implemented policies and procedures
3. Led by one (or more) toxic leaders
4. Negative communication patterns
5. Personal life negatively affected on many fronts

Though the magnitude of the problem is greater than that of having a toxic boss, the best solution is still the same: Move on as quickly as possible. Plan B is the same as well: Go to the literature for help and to your support network for cultivating dignity.

Rule 10: Do Not Forget Rules 1 to 9

Obviously these rules are not the end of the boss-managing road. But they will help you develop a thoughtful plan for proactive interaction with the boss that will minimize unnecessary roadblocks to achieving work through others.

MANAGING YOUR PEERS AND EXTERNAL NETWORKS

Your peers are those within your organization, and they fall into two general groups: those who occupy positions similar or identical to yours, regardless of their level on the organizational staircase; and those who occupy positions different from yours, such as IT staff and support staff. In addition to treating peers with respect and expressing appreciation for their contribution to the organization, practice seeing each person as an end, rather than as a means to some end of yours. Make sure that you are cultivating genuine and authentic but professional relationships. Naturally, it's a difficult balance to maintain—building relationships with your peers but also hoping that they will support requests that you make. The balancing act is worth the effort, though. Not only does it boost morale and strengthen a frayed social fabric, but it makes it possible for you to request assistance from others without using them.

Relationships to Build

Managing peers involves securing cooperation, follow-through, and execution from those in the organization over whom you have no direct authority. Their cooperation is, in a sense, voluntary, although they need you as well. Since they all pertain to managing people, the recommendations for managing yourself and your boss can also be adapted and applied to managing your peers. Your colleagues may have some toxic traits as may you yourself. Connect on a regular basis—for coffee, lunch, a chat—especially with professional peers, and especially when you don't need anything from them. Find out how they are doing and if they could use any help from you. An offer of help is worth a lot, even if they do not need it. This authentic, positive connectivity increases the likelihood that they will be willing to support you when you need assistance, follow-through, and execution from them.

Moreover, these interactions also allow you to update peers on what you are doing and how it might impact them. Most community benefit organizations have limited formal systems for gathering and sharing organizational intelligence; therefore, much information passes through the informal system. Letting coworkers know that your project might have some impact on what they are doing keeps them in the loop. They in turn are likely to let you know when what they are doing might affect you.

Relationships to Avoid

Some peer relationships are better avoided, but how can you tell the difference between helpful and harmful relationships, particularly if you are new to an organization? One perennial rule of thumb is to keep a sharp eye out for quid pro quo relationships—those based solely on the exchange of favors. Vidich and Bensman (1958) explored the age-old assumption that small towns are friendlier than big cities and that it was easy, in a small town, to borrow a proverbial cup of sugar from one's next-door neighbor. They found that this assumption was, like many, only part of the story. You could easily borrow a cup of sugar in a small town. But citizens also remembered that you had borrowed, and they expected you would repay. However, the terms of social borrowing and repaying are vague—you may be implicitly expected to repay with interest, or in a different currency than the one in which you borrowed, or at a time different from the one you had planned. Organizations are a lot like small towns: They keep track of social debit and credit. People notice how much you draw out, how much you put in, and how you put it in, and they transfer this information via the informal organizational structure.

One variation of quid pro quo is evidenced by the "HiHowAreYa" colleague. All organizations have them—the people who never reach out unless they want something. But, when they do, they could not be friendlier, closer, or warmer—because they want something from you. Unfortunately, when you need their help, they are far less warm and welcoming and far less able to commit. A second variation is the "What's In It For Me?" person. These colleagues will help you, but they want immediate payback, with interest. A third is the person who is willing to help—but on his or her own terms, not the terms you need. Some help is really a hindrance and can actually set you back.

As we spend time in organizations, we develop reputations as colleagues. We are continually rated in some invisible sociological amalgam that takes in all our contributions, positive and negative, and spits out a reputation. We can change them. But, make no mistake, we all have them, and we all use them. While you can't control this mysterious algorithm, do strive to be personable, empathic, genuine—and, even when the stakes are high, not mercenary. In turn, chances are high that your close network of "trustys," "dependables," or whatever you want to call them, whom you help and on whom you can call for help, is solid, healthy, and growing.

MANAGING YOUR EXTERNAL NETWORK

The same insights that apply to managing peers are relevant to managing your external network. Building a network outside, as well as inside, the organization is vital to your professional health. It is good to have a "community cabinet," a cadre outside the organization with whom you connect on a regular basis. Your peers, staff, and boss are all immersed in the culture of the organization. Thus, take care to cultivate relationships outside of your organization, and even outside of your particular sector, since industries and professions share assumptions across organizations. Your community cabinet might include friends; external colleagues; your priest, minister, rabbi, or coach; your spouse or partner (careful here—they are your fiercest allies, but they often have an ax to grind if a demanding boss or toxic organization is taking a toll on you); and others in whom you have confidence. Your aim in cultivating such relationships is to develop and invest your social capital.

One important difference between managing internal peers and external networks: When managing internal peers, you often begin by cultivating relationships and then bring an issue together around those with whom you've built relationships. When managing external networks, you tend to start with an issue and bring people together to address it. Issues are complex—to address them you often collaborate and coordinate with multiple external people and organizations (and thus temperaments and agendas and cultures). To successfully manage an issue with your external network, you need to consider, in addition to personalities and priorities, the following elements of issue management and leadership: bundling, framing, and involvement. These may seem more complicated than they really are. I am just naming things that many—most—readers already do.

One issue management and leadership technique is *bundling*. Bundling refers to the actual package of issue elements you include or do not include in your issue package. You are thinking here about what kind of people might sign on or turn off depending upon what piece is in (or is not in) the issue package that you present.

A second technique is *framing*, which refers to the way in which you make the case for their involvement (or for them to "stay out of this one"). It means articulating both the business and cultural reasons that should guide their decisions. These need to be thought out in advance because it is hard to be creative on the spot.

A third technique is *involvement*. At what point in the issue development process do you involve other stakeholders, and which stakeholders, and how intensively? One thing to keep in mind is the concept of "buy-in." We have all heard managers say that they need to get "buy-in" from the community, from other professionals, whatever. However, all too often the issue is bundled and framed and *then* buy-in is sought. It is good to keep in mind that, after all, this is the country of the Boston Tea Party and the idea of "No Taxation without Representation." Buy-in requires build-in; if stakeholders are involved at the front end, the back end is much more pleasant. This sounds so simple. But managing expectations and understanding where your stakeholders are coming from allows you to customize and tailor your proposals and ideas to fit person and culture.

CONCLUSION

Far from being the sine qua non of management and leadership, the exercise of power is a complicating factor. It depends in large part on the subordinate recognizing and submitting to that authority. Moreover, it rests on a foundation of threat and/or infliction of pain. These breed resentment, are costly, and can be ineffective if the subordinate does not fear them. Hence, even where authority is present, master managers find that seeking authentic cooperation and commitment is a wise course. Learning to manage from the "second" position, then, is the job of an effective manager. Generally, each of these techniques can be considered "leading from the second position" (Kanter, 1982), and they lead to situations in which power is ambiguous. In many ways this ambiguity is a good thing, because successful management and leadership, the art of achieving work through others, is more reliably grounded in influence than authoritarian exercise of power.

REFLECTION

- Using the framework provided in this chapter, construct a "tip sheet" on how to best manage your boss. Take into consideration his or her communication style, position in the organization, reputation needs, and physical/mental health.
- Who is in your peer network? What general categories do your peers fall into (HiHowAreYa, etc.)
- Who is in your external network? Which relationships are particularly important to cultivate? Why?
- Is your use of *bundling, framing,* and *involvement* implicit (done without thinking about it) or explicit (intentional, planned)? Describe one issue that required you to use these techniques and the result.

FURTHER READING

Ferazzi, K. (2009). *Who's got your back.* New York, NY: Crown Business.

Grant, A. (2014). *Give and take: Why helping others drives our success.* New York, NY: Penguin Books.

Lubit, R. (2003). *Coping with toxic managers, subordinates and other difficult people: Using emotional intelligence to survive and prosper.* Upper Saddle River, NJ: FT Prentice Hall.

Sutton, R. (2012). *Good Boss, bad boss.* New York, NY: Business Plus.

Sutton, R. (2017). *The asshole survival guide.* New York, NY: Houghton Mifflin Harcourt.

White, P., Chapman, G., & Myra, H. (2014). *Rising above a toxic workplace.* Chicago, IL: Northfield.

PART 4

The Product Picture

Accomplishing Jobs, Tasks, and Work

This volume does not question the foundations of organizational structure, culture, management, or leadership, but it does synthesize efforts to identify them and the best practices that stem from navigating them successfully. I hope that this gives you the tools to understand why recommended practices are indeed good practices—without sacrificing readability or practitioner focus.

In reality, managing people and outputs/outcomes are inseparable. In part 3, for the sake of clarity, we "bracketed" the personnel aspect of management and leadership, so that we could examine it more closely. Now we do the same with *jobs, tasks, projects,* and *work*—terms of art that help us specifically examine the types of outputs and outcomes that lead to lasting impact and accomplished missions.

To get at these concepts, we move from narrow to broad concepts: Chapter 10 focuses on jobs; chapter 11 explores tasks and projects; and chapter 12 examines work. As we proceed, keep in mind (perhaps using Table P4.1) what we've learned regarding organizations, managers, and managing people. Our focus in this part of the book is on columns 3, 4, and 5 of Table P4.1.

Table P4.1. Supervisory/Managerial Focus

Supervisory/Managerial People Focus		Supervisory/Managerial Product Focus		
Management Target	*Managing*	*Tasks*	*Projects*	*Systems/ Mission*
Yourself (and family)	In (within)	X	X	X
Your subordinates (direct reports)	Down	X	X	X
Your peers	Across		X	X
Your bosses	Up			X
Your external network	Out			X

10

Managing Jobs

INTRODUCTION

Most managers think that supervision begins when they are given a person to "boss." But, as we established in chapter 7, you are your first direct report. Supervision and management really begin when you are given a job, which is why self-supervision is so important. But whether you have yourself, alone, or several other direct reports, you essentially have three foci and are accountable for achieving success in three areas: the *job*, the *assignments within the job*, and *completion of the assignments*.

ASSIGNMENTS: THE ESSENTIAL JOB

When you and/or a supervisee are new, these job descriptions are wish lists that almost no one could realistically complete, and they often end with the laconic "other duties as assigned." When you or your supervisee have been with the organization for some time, the description may have meandered and become vague, unclear, unfocused. It is perhaps better to call it a "job scaffolding," the broad framework under which your job is constructed. So your first responsibility is to understand the job and extract its essential components from the unwieldy job description.

To understand the essential job, you need to ask yourself a range of questions, among them: What does the description mean to me? What does it mean to the boss? How does it relate to the organizational mission? Who benefits (e.g., who are the stakeholders, the audience, the customers)? What are the time/money budget constraints? This is true whether the supervisee is yourself or a direct report. As you extract, you select out of all the jobs in the description, the package to which you must attend (if managing yourself), or the package to which you want your staff to attend. Usually, this process is one of negotiation, in which you have priorities. Staff often have some interests as well, some, but not all, of which may align with your own and require compromise.

Your second responsibility is identifying and clarifying the weights or time emphasis that you expect to be allocated to the work and/or in which you expect the work to be done. This is called the *effort ratio*, the proportion of your time to be spent on each aspect of the essential job. Failure to articulate these weights is a huge source of misunderstanding. The Index of Difference (Table 7.1) is helpful for assessing the weights and their differences (if any) between you and your staff or you and your boss.

OVERSIGHT: THE MEANS/ENDS CHAIN

Your third responsibility is to ensure that the assignments within the job are completed on time and on budget and that they are of high quality in both process (means) and outcome (ends). This dual focus on quality means and ends is always important, but quality thinkers approach them differently. Some think that a quality process always produces a quality outcome; therefore unsatisfactory outcomes are the result of problems in previous processes.

There is truth in this assertion, but it misses two essential components. First, external factors, which the process did not consider, may influence outcomes. However, some might say, the failure to anticipate those variables is a failure of process. Fine, but "things" happen whether you plan for them or not—including effacement in budgetary allocation with no parallel change in responsibility, governmental changes, and global terror events. Any one of these is enough to throw the best-planned process into disarray. Second, sometimes people do fail to anticipate all the internal elements that could create roadblocks for success. For example, managers might rely on a certain motivation level of staff, one similar to their own, only to find that staff are really not as motivated for project success as the manager is.

To ensure quality means and ends, managers must oversee both. To ignore process and focus on results invites manipulation of the process to produce the desired results, often at questionable quality. To ignore outcomes on the assumption that proper means will produce proper ends ignores external and internal change, which can make an excellent product or the outcome irrelevant. Outcomes are nested in a means-ends chain. Managers must check into that chain at various points to be sure that means and ends are functioning and synchronous. "A chain is only as strong as its weakest link" applies to the means-ends chain as well. Hence, managers must find out where the most vulnerable and critical areas of the chain are and pay special attention to those points. In performing these checks, the manager must seek a middle, a way of attending to both means and ends. Managers themselves can influence quality: If they have no feel for what's happening on the ground, or are too close to the ground to see the larger picture, they demotivate staff, dampen creativity and improvement, and substantively contribute to poor quality.

QUALITY: UNACCEPTABLE, ACCEPTABLE, BETTER, BEST, AND EXCEPTIONAL

A routine and regular operation of the means-ends chain will produce outcomes of acceptable quality. But clearly defining acceptable quality is very hard, especially in community benefit organizations, which focus on the Sisyphean task of mitigating wicked problems. This difficulty brings to light your fourth responsibility: defining acceptable performance in terms that you and your staff agree on. But you should not stop at clarifying acceptable/unacceptable. Acceptable is good, but there is still room for exploring better, best, and exceptional. *Good* is the minimum performance level. *Better* and *best* are achievable goals. *Exceptional* is always a possibility.

Moreover, *customer* has many meanings, ranging from the service user outside of your organization to people you assist or support within your organization, to your family members. In fact, anyone downstream from you can be considered your customer. As a thoughtful manager, you want to aim to offer your best and inspire those you work with to give their best, to the whole range of customers, every day.

CONCLUSION

In this chapter, we explored the nuts and bolts of managing jobs: what it takes to extract the essential job from an unwieldy job description; how to create an effort ratio; and how to set performance expectations as a way to ensure movement toward quality. This very basic examination will help us as we move from an examination of jobs to the tasks and projects that they comprise.

REFLECTION

- In a staff meeting, review your organization's service record (or your personal service to customers) using this grading schema. How "good" (really) is your service? How do you know? Would customers corroborate your insight if asked?

FURTHER READING

Snow, D., & Yanovitch, T. (2009). *Unleashing excellence: The complete guide to ultimate customer service* (2nd ed.). Hoboken, NJ: Wiley.
Sostrin, J. (2013). *Beyond the job description: How managers and employees can navigate the true demands of the job.* New York, NY: Palgrave Macmillan.

11

Managing Tasks and Projects

INTRODUCTION

While all managers by training *react* to circumstances—those inevitable instances of Murphy's Law—better managers and leaders anticipate circumstances before they occur. But the best managers and leaders conceptualize and act so effectively that neither internal nor external constituencies see the preparation and effort required. The managerial performance is seamless. In this chapter, we examine the responsibilities and priorities of such a project manager, who retains all responsibilities for supervision assigned at the previous level while taking on the responsibility for management of tasks and projects.

The project manager develops two sets of skills in terms of the project itself. One is task assembly, sequencing and orchestration. The second is execution. Task assembly involves putting together the relevant parts of jobs into task bundles and then ordering the bundles so that their completion, one after the other, leads to project completion, within the parameters of time and budget. The process of accomplishing, bundling, and sequencing is called orchestration.

The manager also needs to conceptualize the project (have ideas about it) so that there is an overarching frame of reference into which elements and parts fit. Decisions about problems and potential problems need to be made in a timely manner. And once those decisions are made, there needs to be execution—the part that actually makes things happen. This step is more complex for three reasons.

1. *Tasks* are composed of collections of parts of jobs. You have to be aware of a greater range of factors inside and outside of the organization.
2. *Projects* are composed of bundles and batches of assignments. A range of people and competencies are involved. They must be orchestrated, which means that you, like a conductor, know the score.
3. *Project management* requires you to be significantly more aware of factors and events outside of your project that may affect your work. Religious holidays, for example, can affect scheduling.

While we can't cover all aspects of project management (again, a discipline that merits volumes), we do focus here on several important essential principles:

1. Understanding project orchestration
2. Understanding events and activities
3. Understanding the allocation of managerial energy
4. Understanding ideas (that lead to) decisions (that lead to) implementation
5. Understanding project management organizational tools
   a. Logic Modeling
   b. Gantt Charting
   c. PERT Charting
6. Tips for project management/leadership

TASK-PROJECT ORCHESTRATION

A project is a set of interrelated tasks, bound by dates and deliverables and designed to accomplish a mission or goal. These sets of tasks exist over time and may involve a range of players. Project managers bring together people, equipment, other resources, and jobs to complete tasks. Task bundles are assembled in batches and then strung together to form a string of tasks and, when completed, result in the product. Both bundles and batches need to be carefully managed.

The bundles need to be formed/melded into coherent batches. These batches, in turn, need to be sequenced appropriately so that the desired outcome (deliverable) can be achieved by the desired time (date). The term *project* is a way to refer to the whole package of task bundles, usually named after or referring to the end product, such as "planning the annual meeting." Orchestration addresses the managerial issue of ordering, sequencing, tempo, entrances and exits of parts, and elements, which all need to work synchronously in order for the product to be produced on time, in budget, with the outcome to be achieved. Orchestration is the process through which tasks coalesce into projects and achieve completion.

PARTS AND ELEMENTS

Tasks have both parts and elements. *Parts,* temporally and functionally discrete jobs, start and finish at some point within the project process and accomplish some subgoal. They may reappear at various intervals throughout the project (e.g., quarterly budget reviews), but they do start and stop. *Elements,* on the other hand, are ongoing and occur throughout the life of the project (environmental scanning, etc.). Project managers oversee a project's episodic parts and its ongoing elements.

EVENTS AND ACTIVITIES

Activities connect events. *Events* are milestones, the completion of a task bundle (submitting an application). *Activities* are the period between the completion of one task bundle and the beginning of another (waiting for an RFP to be issued). If a project is like a link of sausages, each sausage is an event and the linkages are the activities.

MANAGEMENT PERSPECTIVES: ALLOCATING MANAGERIAL ENERGY

Project managers superintend the parts, elements, events, and activities that make up a project. Most projects have a repetitive aspect in which "local knowledge" helps staff to self-manage. However, managers—especially those who are trying to more vigorously apply the skills from their old job to the demands of the new job—often make the mistake of "managing" (intruding on) effective processes and failing to apply energy to areas of need. Generally, managers need to encourage the steady pace of the routine and regular while simultaneously managing the exceptions.

Each project manager has somewhat different expectations for routine and regular functions like pace, cost, and quality. They do vary within these (and other) parameters, and addressing them is part (a big part) of the manager's job since most quality problems come from system failures—problems within the routine and the regular that managers have neglected.

These exceptions to routine and regular processes often expand later in the project cycle. Managing the exceptions means attending to smaller problems earlier in the process, if possible, so that they do not mushroom and disrupt other areas. A project is like a small stream. A branch removed does not interrupt the flow of water. If left to float downstream, though, chances are it will catch on a rock, snag other branches and leaves, and possibly dam the whole works. Similarly, in project management and leadership, problems build on each other. If they are addressed in a timely fashion, the project proceeds unhindered.

As a general rule, it is often helpful to attend to the opposite of what is going well at the moment. If one aspect of the project is going well, devote your energy to the aspect that isn't. If management of persons and products seems to be well in hand, take a step back and consider whether shifting your focus to leadership issues will benefit the organization, mission, team, or project. A second helpful rule is to gauge your experience and competence over against that of your project team. Some staff will be old hands at the responsibilities within their jurisdiction, and they will require remarkably little oversight. Some may need training or coaching. Make sure that you have a clear sense of who needs you to check in with them and who needs you to check up on them.

IDEAS, DECISIONS, AND EXECUTION

In this section we touch on three essential "KSAs" (knowledge, skills, and abilities) needed for an effective perspective on project management: ideas, decisions, and execution.

A manager needs to conceptualize, or have ideas about, the flow of the project in order to anticipate sequences, likelihoods, blockages, chokepoints, interdependencies, and simultaneities. A manager also should have ideas about the content of each component and the time required to complete them. Will component C be ready when component B shows up? He or she also needs to conceptualize and anticipate externalities. What elements outside the project (other projects, for example) might impede timely progress? In short, the manager needs to conceptualize the entire project and its components, like an orchestra conductor conceptualizes an entire sonata and all of its subsections, or like a chef conceptualizes a menu. This conceptualizing is the first aspect of project management.

Project conceptualization is the ability to see the whole project, event, dinner, or performance in its entirety. Conceptualization involves a manager who is able to see both the parts and the elements, the events and activities, which will be needed to make it succeed, as well as their sequences and interdependency. The second skill, component time estimation, simply involves a good sense of how long it will take to complete A so that we know when to schedule B, so that in turn we know when to schedule C, and so on. Both these skills involve not only knowing the event but also the necessary activities that lead up to the event.

Drawing on the work of conceptualization, managers then need to make decisions. A decision, as we said earlier, is drawing a conclusion about a plan of action. Decisions range in scope and complexity, depending on the nature of the project. Categories of project-related decisions may include plans such as staff assignments, milestones, goal dates, budget allocations, and others. Making good decisions is such an indispensable part of management that we explore it at length in chapter 14.

We have all experienced managers who are unable to decide anything. They seem paralyzed by the possibilities and respond like the proverbial deer in the headlights. Some pathological managers are unable to hold to a decision, changing strategic direction and scrapping operational plans as their moods and anxieties wax and wane. The pokey decision-maker is "too little too late," and his or her opposite number takes the "fire, ready, aim" approach. Decision paralysis, decision waffling, and decision pre- and post-maturity are equally damaging to projects.

Following conceptualization and decision-making, managers have to execute. They have to make, cause, and arrange for the plan to happen. We are culturally predisposed to divide people into two groups: those who make things happen and those who do not. We all know people who, when they say they are going to invite you over, actually do invite you over; who say "let's vacation in the Adirondacks" and actually make the arrangements. In other words, when they say they are going to do something, anything, actually *do* that thing. Ideally, project managers should come from the first group, of course. In the execution phase, project managers create results and outcomes, achieve objectives and milestones, or enable others to achieve them. Execution differs from, but builds on, conceptualization and decision-making. Using previous work, managers engage with, but refrain from micromanaging all aspects of the project so that it actually happens. While they might take on responsibility for completing some aspect of the project, they more often keep a bird's-eye view, managing the exceptions (i.e., doing a little bit of many different tasks) so that their staff has as few hindrances as possible and are motivated to work hard and finish well. Managers who execute well tend to display a common set of characteristics:

1. They initiate, and stick to, a course of action, absorbing feedback and implementing course corrections at planned intervals.
2. They cultivate staff productivity by minimizing possible demotivators (including but not limited to unmanaged exceptions, mismatch between expectations and resources, lack of staff training, incoherence between formal and nonverbal/informal communication) and maximizing team coherence (clear communication, appropriate praise and recognition, setting a brisk but manageable project pace).
3. They attend to, but do not seek to manage, every detail of the project.

PROJECT MANAGEMENT COMMUNICATION TOOLS

Project communication involves writing down and posting the "plan" so that all involved can know what their responsibilities are and the time frames in which they have to work. It is amazing how many project managers conceptualize and make decisions about the project and then fail to inform others of the "plan," rendering their work on earlier steps essentially useless.

Project managers are responsible for keeping the project on schedule, which is why well-honed conceptualization, decision-making, and execution skills are absolutely nonnegotiable. Wise managers also enlist the support of staff in keeping the project on schedule, and they often use a formal tool—such as a logic model, a Gantt chart, or a PERT chart to share the schedule with staff and communicate progress, updates, and areas of concern. We discuss each next. First, though, consider the following checklist for achieving a useful schedule.

✓ Begin with your end goal in mind
✓ Identify all events and activities needed to achieve end goal
✓ Specify the details of all events and activities
✓ Determine the resources needed for each event and activity
✓ Specify the person resources needed for each event and activity by KSI

✓ Assess the material and human resources you have available

✓ Elicit and spell out assumptions that you and each team member hold

✓ Review your tentative schedule following project approval and prior to project start

✓ Identify the potential implications of other ongoing projects and activities

✓ Develop contingency plans for high-risk components

✓ Revise estimates, if necessary, after people have been assigned to your team

Logic Modeling: Dates and Deliverables

A logic model shows an orderly progression, from start to finish, of a project's components. These usually include the following elements.

Inputs
Processes
Outputs
Short-term outcomes
Intermediate outcomes
Long-term outcomes

Consider a logic model of the adoption process. Inputs consist of children and potential parents, as well as various resources and staff the agency might have (there are other routes to adoption other than a child welfare agency, but the child welfare agency is the focus here). Processes are the steps the agency creates for the child, the adoptive parents, and relevant others (natural mom, dad, etc.) on the way to the adoption finalization. These may include visits, working out arrangements with the natural mom, and so on. An output would be the finalization of the adoption. An outcome would be a positive result for parents and child. The short-term outcomes would be those that happen immediately after the adoption, such as adjustment in the first year; long-term outcomes might include the child growing up to be an adult who can love and work.

Flow Charting

Another way to visually display the flow of work is through a flow chart. A flow chart has a set of common symbols, and it is a more detailed analysis of work processes than logic models. The logic model contains some elements (outcomes, outputs) that the flow chart does not, and the flow chart has more different kinds of work processes than the logic model. The flow chart is also useful for analyzing work processes, as well as planning them. In the analysis application, steps, action points, and decisions may be found to be redundant and can be taken out of the system, simplifying it. This is called *workout,* taking work out of the system.

Gantt Charting

After developing a logic model, move on to Gantt charting. Developed by Henry Gantt in the 1910s, Gantt charting builds on the soup-to-nuts list of elements, adding start, duration, and finish times to outputs and outcomes, if desired.

This task requires the project manager to conceptualize, at a more specific level, what each component of the project needs and when. Once these questions have an answer, the project manager can begin to list and compile resources that will be needed to meet these event milestones. The Gantt chart provides a visual tool for managers and project team members to track what task will be going on during each phase of the project. The first example (Figure 11.1) shows that Task A is an initiating task, but it ends prior to the completion of the goal, whereas Task C will run for almost the duration of the project. Task D, in this example, will only occur in the completion phase. This example is taken from everyday life and depicts how the goal of purchasing a new car can be divided up into four general tasks. Before you know what to buy you have to first know what you can afford to buy, which in this case is determined during the first month of the process. Task C, negotiating with dealers and lenders, is part of months 2 to 4, as it is an integral and ongoing part of the goal of buying a car (see Figure 11.1).

In the next example from the Gantt chart, we lay out a procedure for manager/leaders who are assigning new cases. This is because every task is assigned to a time frame, which allows managers/supervisors to answer the questions "What do we need?" and "When do we need it?" For example, in a social service setting, the manager can use Gantt charting with workers for each case in their caseload. When supervisors and staff sit down together, the Gantt chart review is an excellent way for them to mutually chart case tasks, assess case progress, and determine

A. Calculate budget				
B. Research and test drive				
C. Negotiate				
D. Financing and Purchasing				
Month	1	2	3	4

Figure 11.1 The product picture.

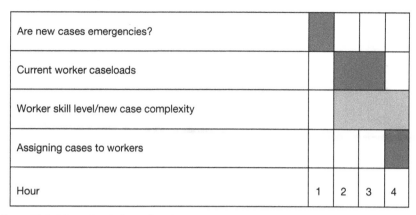

	1	2	3	4
Are new cases emergencies?				
Current worker caseloads				
Worker skill level/new case complexity				
Assigning cases to workers				
Hour	1	2	3	4

Figure 11.2 Managing tasks and projects.

where simultaneity of activities lies and in what time frames. If the Gantt chart is employed with individual cases (see Figure 11.2), there will be commonalities among tasks and time frames, although the needs of individual families and children must be taken into account.

PERT Charting

Originally developed for the construction of the nuclear submarine fleet, PERT charting is useful for very complex tasks with varying timelines and interdependencies, such as a capital campaign, a major agency reorganization, and so on. PERT, which stands for Program, Evaluation and Review Technique, is a way to identify and track project activities over time. Key concepts in PERT charting include the following:

Events and activities
Predecessor and successor events; simultaneous events
Time estimation (an activity has a *Te*, an expected time, and a *Tm*, a
    maximum time)
Critical path ($Te = Tm$)
Slack ($Te < Tm$)

When Gantt charting, you develop a list of *events*, milestones or actions at one point in time, and *activities*, actions occurring over time. In the Gantt chart, activities are represented by a bar. Shorter bar length means shorter activities; longer bar length means longer activities. Each activity has two events associated with it: initiating and terminating, the points where the bar begins and ends.

As in the Gantt, events in the PERT chart have a sequence that the project manager must follow so that the project can be completed. The first step in developing a PERT chart, which is largely completed by constructing a Gantt, is to make a

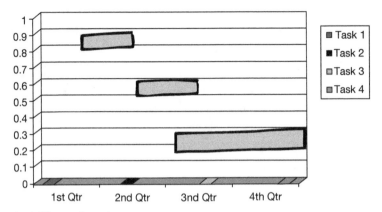

Figure 11.3 The product picture.

two-column list of events and activities needed to complete the project. Often it is good to jot events and activities on post-its—one event or activity on each—so that the chronological order of events and activities can be easily changed. Often, as we review the initial chronological order of project events and activities, we see that we have them wrong or that it would be better to do something earlier (or later) than we had originally thought, and we need to change the order of events and activities. Using post-its makes it easy to do so. Simultaneous events means that events are "stacked." See the simple PERT in Figure 11.3. for reference.

TERMINATING EVENT

The next phase of PERTing is to lay out activities and events across a time-line, again much like in a Gantt. In PERT charts, you use arrows instead of bars to represent activities. Above each, in about the middle, there is a little symbol, *Te* =, which stands for "estimated time equals." The number following the = sign is the estimated time it will take to the complete activity and corresponds to the amount of space the line occupies on the base time below. Below the line is another *Tm* =, which indicates the maximum amount of time the activity can take. For example, suppose you were driving from Smithville to Greenston, which takes about one hour, and you need to be there by 4 PM for a meeting. If you leave at 2:30, you could arrive half an hour early, it all goes well. In this case *Te* > *Tm*. If you leave at 3 PM exactly, *Te* = *Tm*. If you leave at 3:15, then *Te* < *Tm*. In the first case, you have "slack" or extra time to play with in case something comes up. In the second case, you have the so-called critical path or no-slack path. In the third case, you have "crisis" because you have started too late, really have no chance of making the meeting, and might be tempted to use potentially problematic approaches (speeding, comer cutting) to make the meeting.

SOME TIPS FOR TASK AND PROJECT MANAGEMENT AND LEADERSHIP

Supervisors, project managers, and middle managers need to be aware of a range of factors in task and project management and leadership. Portney (2000) lists these, and I have added some explanations where feedback indicates that they might not be self-evident. These are useful to keep in mind:

- Avoiding common pitfalls
- Developing meaningful business objectives
- Developing achievable schedules
- Improving your personal estimates
- Eliciting and sustaining commitment
- Communicating effectively

Each area contains a set of bullets that alert managers to issues. I have selected *Common Pitfalls, Meaningful Objectives,* and *Eliciting and Sustaining Commitment* as most relevant here.

Avoiding Common Project Pitfalls

Most tasks bundles and projects run into trouble because of the common, rather than the uncommon, issues and problems. These are useful to review and keep in mind. A few are listed in Table 11.1.

Developing Meaningful Objectives

As the common phrase has it, "If you do not know where you are going, any road will take you there." Crisp, understandable objectives are crucial. Outcomes, rather than activities or outputs, are the name of the game; outcomes would be client improvement, for example, rather than interviews held; jobs secured for clients rather than referrals made; customer/client/consumer satisfaction rather than meetings. See Table 11.2.

Eliciting and Sustaining Commitment

Motivation and commitment to a project is something that, to some extent, workers bring to the job. People come to work for nonprofits because they believe in and are passionate about the mission that organization embodies, whether it

Table 11.1. Avoiding Common Project Problems

Common Problem	Tropman's Insight
Settling for unclear goals	Nail these down.
Failing to clarify your assumptions, commitments, and audiences	Do an audit of assumptions, a separate audit of commitments, and a third audit of audiences/stakeholders. Put these in writing and ask for a second (and third) set of eyes.
Incohesive teams that lack identity, purpose, and commitment	Give your team a name. Spend time defining and refining the team's identity and purpose. Using the SMART format, make explicit the commitments needed. Commit to reviewing these as a team at set intervals throughout the life of the project.
Insufficient accountability structures	Tough to do but essential. If they cannot/do not deliver, they lack integrity and should move along.
Indecisive project schedules	This happens when you let the situations drive the schedules, rather than developing schedules at the front end. Build a schedule before you begin.
Insufficient benchmarks and check-in points	Establish SMART aims and then commit to "inspect what you expect."
No formal risk identification and management	Attend to the critical paths. Ask yourself where things could really "crash."
Poor communications	Overcommunicate. Use both written and verbal channels.
No organized method for introducing and evaluating requested changes	Determine what method you will use to address and evaluate suggestions for change. Outline procedures for implementing change in project flow and associated documents.
Failure to learn from past project lessons	Complete an after-action report and lessons-learned document.

is children's services or band, art, or dance camp. However, commitment is like a houseplant: It may arrive healthy but it needs to be cared for and sustained. Managers need to be a "constant gardener of that commitment, freeing it from weeds and providing it with nourishment." Suggestions for this are included in Table 11.3.

ENHANCING PEOPLE'S PERFORMANCE

The manager needs to increase team cohesion through an appropriate mix of professional and personal connections. Professional connections are comprised of effective, dignity-enhancing supervision, management, and leadership. Personal

Table 11.2. How to Arrive at Clear Project Aims (And Avoid Mission Creep)

	Steps in the Process	Tropman's Insights
1	Attend to the desired outcomes.	Ask yourself, "at the end of this project, what specific activities will the team have done?"
2	Use plain language.	Obfuscatory, polysyllabic verbiage must of necessity be replaced with clear, active, precise, one-syllable words.
3	Determine how you'll measure each aim.	Measures are things like miles per hour, satisfaction scores, number of contacts in a week, etc.
4	Identify one specific performance target for each measure.	Targets are outcomes that each aim must achieve, for example, miles per day completed, contacts per week reached, etc.
5	Identify a specific time frame for each aim.	Attach time frames for completion to each aim. Rate of progress or date of completion or some mixture of both is fine. But if no time is attached, the aim may drag on, and on, and on, and on, without reaching completion.
6	Plan achievable aims.	Be realistic. "Stretch" aims (what you achieved previously, plus a bit more) usually work. However, if aims are not achievable, staff see them as a tool of management to "speed up the line." Impossible aims provoke corner-cutting. They encourage staff to game the system, lie about progress, or cheat on process.
7	Make all aims explicit, and ensure that all expectations are explicit.	Be the locus of communication. Most projects are a loosely connected group of people pursuing discrete but interrelated aims. Be trustworthy, stay in contact with each member of the team, and elicit frank feedback about aims and expectations.

Table 11.3. How Do You Cultivate and Sustain Team Commitment to a Project?

Guiding Questions to Inform Best Practices	Tropman's Insights
How will your project benefit team members?	Constantly discuss the relationship between larger goals and personal goals.
Can you involve team members in planning? How?	Involvement in problem-solving hastens technical solutions and builds emotional satisfaction.
Have you demonstrated or explained (effectively) how and why your plan is do-able?	Part fact, part faith. This is the role of the project leader. Encouragement plus practicality. Casting a vision and adhering to careful project metrics will support team and stakeholder understanding of the plan.
Do you know how to address issues, concerns, and questions promptly and openly, using a solution-oriented approach?	Hold regular meetings that identify issues to be resolved, workarounds to build, and decisions to make. Avoid newsletter meetings.
What is consistent, substantive feedback in the context of your project? How will you share it?	Use meetings for problem sharing and feedback securing. Involve the whole team in feedback sessions.
What mechanism(s) do you have in place to recognize team member contributions? Are these effective in your context?	Have a team "ego wall." This can be an overall measure like the thermometer the United Way uses during its campaigns; posted achievements of subunits and congratulatory notes or emails are also useful.
Do team members know one another? How can you foster authentic relationships?	Host informal events for the team.
What is your approach to focusing on your team members' strengths rather than their limitations?	Worry less about what is left out and strengthen what is left in.

Table 11.4. A Gantt Chart

Task				
A				
B				
C				
D				
E				
Time Frame	1	2	3	4

connections are informal meetings with staff—perhaps breakfast or lunch where anyone can join and talk—so that the team or staff can get to know the manager as a person, not merely as a professional. Personal connections may also involve occasional hosting and other kinds of social interaction.

CONCLUSION

Because they have mastered (or are mastering) the perspectives and skills discussed in this chapter, the very best managers are always a step ahead; their presence is unnoticed because the product is so good. Making things happen, or helping things to happen, or encouraging things to happen is a skill unto itself. We all know lots of people who have great plans but can never bring anything to fruition. We also know people who make things happen, but they are often the wrong things. In this chapter, we have examined skills project managers can cultivate to ensure that they develop and execute exceptional, and effective, projects.

REFLECTION

Planning with Gantt
- A sample blank Gantt template appears as Table 11.4. What small projects can you plan and organize using the Gantt?

Thinking Ahead
- What pitfalls do tasks and projects encounter in your organization?
- How do you or other managerial staff typically handle them when they arise?
- List two very practical ways that you or other managerial staff can begin to manage "downstream," so that you clear those blockages or mend the pitfalls before the project encounters them.

FURTHER READING

Project Management Introductions

Kogon, K., Wood, J., & Blakemore, S. (2015). *Project management for the unofficial project manager.* Dallas, TX: BenBella Books.

Portny, S. (2017). *Project management for dummies* (5th ed.). Hoboken, NJ: Wiley.

Project Management Communication

Logic Model Development Guide. (n.d.) www.wkkf.org/resource-directory/resource/2006/02/wk-kellogg-foundation-logic-model-development-guide

12

Managing Work

INTRODUCTION

While supervisors tend to address the concerns of jobs and project managers address jobs, tasks, and projects, middle managers oversee *work,* a set of projects that, as they succeed, accomplish the mission of the organization and embody and articulate its purpose. Leaders oversee the strategy of the organization. Work, done well, embodies organizational values in such a way that goals are reached through acceptable means. For example, if an organization is set up to serve the poor, and does so, but pays substandard wages to its employees, one group is exploiting another to help another exploited group. The organization may be achieving its outcomes, but the means are unacceptable and the outcomes are diminished. Middle managers are more concerned with effectiveness (doing the right things in the right way) than efficiency (doing things right).

Middle managers retain the responsibilities of previous levels, but they also are responsible to integrate projects so that the organization both meets its commitments and adheres to its community benefit priorities. Take, for example, the old adage, "faster, better, cheaper." These are three competing priorities, and managers of *work* are continually juggling them. How can we work more quickly? How can we produce work of better quality? How can we work less expensively?

Managers also take into account the social context of the organization. In the United States that means that they, and the organizations they serve, are functioning within a deep, and often implicit, cultural structure. This framework prioritizes achievement over equality and airplay over fair share, but it is also riven by the currently ubiquitous questions raised by identity politics. Managers are explicitly charged with keeping their eyes on the prize of successful projects, or work.

Leaders set the overall strategy and are responsible for ensuring that the organization's work aligns with the deep cultural structures within which it functions. Accomplishing the organization's goals, setting appropriate boundaries, and ensuring that employees are adequately resourced and compensated presents three problems for the manager/leader: mission versus margin, wicked problems, and unrealistic expectations.

MANAGING WORK: MISSION VERSUS MARGIN

All organizations have some *mission,* or purpose for existing. In the community benefit sector, providing assistance to and working for the benefit of the community is core to most missions. *Margin* refers to financial stability and profit. In the community benefit organization, it is the manager's job (as well as the job of the CEO and board) to ensure that mission drives the margin, not the other way around. That does not mean that margin does not act as an important boundary. You cannot perform services for which you are not paid, or for which your pay (as occurs in many government contracts) is unilaterally reduced. Moreover, organizations do not offer services that do not align with mission just because they provide margin.

WICKED PROBLEMS

A second problem in community benefit organization work is the fact that the problems tend to be sloppy, poorly defined, and recurring. These types of problems are called wicked problems. A job in a human services organization is one of the most difficult in which to be employed. There are several reasons for this difficulty. I have already outlined a number of them in chapter 6. Here is a recap of that list for easy reference.

1. No definitive formulation.
2. No criteria for determining when the problem is solved.
3. Solutions can be only good/bad, not true/false.
4. No test for whether a proposed solution is a good one.
5. Every solution is a "one-shot" operation. Implementing it makes irreversible changes.
6. There is no exhaustive set of possible solutions or permissible operations.
7. Every wicked problem is unique.
8. Every wicked problem can be a symptom of another problem.
9. People choose explanations for wicked problems that seem plausible to them. Their solutions are shaped by their explanations.
10. Planners have the right to be wrong (but they must take responsibility for their actions).

UNREALISTIC EXPECTATIONS

Adding to this set of pressures, however, is the presence of higher expectations on community benefit executives, relating to the service purpose of their mission. The higher purpose or civic purpose of an organization (nonprofit social service agencies, churches, philanthropies, etc.), may create a stress of its own. We often hope that organizations established to serve the community and to help others would hold to a higher standard. These higher expectations are problematic in their own right. In addition, they may add more complexity because stakeholders tend to think of community benefit organizations and staff as more pure than for-profit organizations and corporate executives and less vulnerable to the range of human venalities. In fact, most community benefit staff, managers, executives, and boards have this view of themselves. If so, the staff and governance structure may rely on these higher expectations and may be less robust and have fewer social/organizational controls that need, apparently, to be always in place and always working.

Another part of this package might be the assumption, perhaps driven by the early domination of human service agencies by volunteers, and their current strong and important presence, that staff members are also a sort of "volunteer." I cannot tell readers how many times I have heard the statement (in my own school of social work as well as many others), "You do not go into human services to make money." While there is a certain truth to this (other motivations are perhaps dominant), the need for a living wage does not go away. And the cliché is often used to excuse insufficient compensation.

In my own case, as an example, I was once interviewed for a deanship of a school of social work at a university in the eastern United States. After two days of meetings, the matter of compensation had still not been brought up. I thought I should initiate conversation about this and asked the woman who was chair of the search committee (and also president of the board of directors) what they were thinking of in terms of compensation. This woman commented, "Well, doctor, at this university, you do not get rich; you get enriched." This mindset is still very prevalent. (By the way, I did not get the offer and was told I was too "pushy" for the culture at that time.)

THE OUTCOMES OF *WORK*

Balancing priorities is not the only responsibility of a manager. He or she must also ensure that the organization produces both product and accomplishment. And, in the high-performing community benefit organization, the manager must ensure that they occur together.

Ensuring Product

In order to ensure *product*, the creation of outcomes, managers must shoulder a range of responsibilities. Not only must the product production must be seamless, regular, dependable, and accountable, but the people assigned to the jobs, tasks, and projects of which product is composed must be well and skillfully led and managed. Specifically, the manager works "along with" the product teams and workers (without micromanaging). Much of what he or she does involves managing by wandering around (MBWA), a constant touching base and querying that gives a sense of the pulse of production across its internal components.

The manager is also in a "feed forward" mode, using current information gleaned from MBWA, plus experience, distilled information from history to work forward, ahead of the product flow, clearing potential obstacles.

In addition to gathering data and managing ahead of project flow, the manager meets more formally with project managers but manager/leaders as well. As the manager meets with the project managers, questions come up that can be addressed now or later, after reflection and checking. If issues come up with supervisors, the manager checks back with the relevant project manager and lets the project manager get back to the supervisor.

Along with these internal activities, managers are managing "out"—checking in with community and other agency stakeholders for important and relevant information. This activity is both a sharing "out" and a bringing "in" of information. Similarly, the manager is managing "up," checking in with the CEO or other members of the top team.

And of course managers also sometimes play "cleanup" as well, working behind the product flow to repair, assuage, and deal with hurt feelings, smooth relationships with stakeholders that were overlooked, and gather any lessons learned to enhance performance in the next round of work.

Ensuring Accomplishment

As mentioned, ensuring product is one of a manager's primary responsibilities. The other is ensuring accomplishment. Accomplishment is something that the staff needs to feel and experience. Staff need appreciation, thanks, recognition, and a constantly vitalized sense of their own importance in the delivery of product. So often, workers in any industry feel unappreciated and unrecognized. Delivering product with a demoralized staff is a sign of managerial failure. And in fact, a demoralized (as opposed to an energized) staff cannot deliver quality product. On the other hand, a staff that feels really good about themselves but does not actually do anything will not feel good for long. Of course, accomplishment creation is even more vital in community benefit organizations, which are immersed in daily efforts to mitigate wicked problems.

Each component of the manager–staff–performance triad experiences *accomplishment* differently. Managers cultivate it by giving attention, caring, listening, treating workers with dignity, and providing adequate resources and compensation. Staff experience accomplishment as it is supported, welcomed, and immersed in an environment that has high expectations (but where they have the resources to meet those expectations). An accomplishment-oriented organization that strikes this balance has a much better chance of high performance across the organization (see Vail's list in the introduction). In contrast, an organization whose staff experiences constrained, inconsistent, or no accomplishment at all is characterized by poor performance, resentment, a pretense of work, high absenteeism, and presenteeism.

A sense of organizational accomplishment can be hindered or impeded by the presence of underperforming individuals. Everyone at work (and we know this to be true from our own experience) knows that there are those within the workforce who are not only not doing their share but are also off-loading work on others. Almost nothing sours workers on their workplace more than to see these individuals consistently "getting away" with this behavior and, even more infuriating, getting rewarded at the same rate of pay. Managing these individuals is a tough job (see chapter 8 for insight on cultivating staff performance). But it is not possible to produce accomplishment and the good feelings that both engender and result from accomplishment while supporting workplace laggards. It is time for these workers to move along.

CONCLUSION

In this chapter, we identified the core responsibility of middle managers as overseeing *work*, the set of projects that prioritize the mission of the organization, without sacrificing accountability to *margin*, or financial stability. For the manager, this requires striking a difficult and shifting balance between explicit responsibilities to mission and margin and implicit responsibilities to align with the priorities of the deep cultural structure within which the organization is embedded. Successful work not only ensures the delivery of a quality product (via quality means) but also ensures the accomplishment of staff—an investment that benefits the organization and shapes the lives of the people who serve in it. In the next part, we turn from the practice of management and leadership of people and product to the communication competencies required to achieve these—regardless of your position in an organization.

REFLECTION

- What is your organization's mission? your team's? What is clear? What is not?
- What kind of margin does it have? How do you know?
- What are the features of the culture in which your organization is embedded?
- How do you ensure staff accomplishment?

FURTHER READING

Marciano, P. (2010). *Carrots and sticks don't work*. New York, NY: McGraw-Hill Education.

Vaill, P. (1989). *Managing as a performing art*. San Francisco, CA: Jossey-Bass.

PART 5

Crosscutting Skills

Competence at Any Level

Because management and leadership involve achieving work through others, managers at every level on the organizational staircase must be competent communicators. (That is, they must have *competence:* knowledge plus skill.) How you apply communication competencies depends on your role, your position, and the specific circumstances, but a strong command of communication competencies is nonnegotiable. They include an efficient (doing things the right way) and effective (doing the right things) grasp of meetings, decision-making, and verbal and written engagement.

The order of competencies is based upon a "complaint gradient" drawn from interviews and consultations with managers and leaders. Meetings get the universal high score of badness. In fact, inefficient, ineffective meetings are so common they have become a sort of national bad joke. Meetings are called, of course, to facilitate decision-making. Organizations rise or fall on the decisions, big or small, the organization makes throughout its structure. Building high-quality decisions is an essential managerial accomplishment. Meetings and decision-making involve writing, and much of what a manager and leader does involves written communication. Polishing that skill—and understanding the range of routine documents and improving them—is important for any manager. Verbal communication involves what you say, how you say it, when you say it, what you omit, and so on.

Volumes, courses, and entire schools exist to help aspiring leaders develop these competencies. In the pages that follow, we sketch a brief outline designed to help you think about and take informed next steps toward flourishing in management and leadership.

13

Producing Effective Meetings

INTRODUCTION

Meetings are the hidden "cost center" of most organizations. The research I have done on meetings suggests that a massive amount of time is wasted in various kinds of useless meetings. And that is only the time in the meeting. When you add the time preparing for, going to, and returning from meetings, the costs in money, energy, and motivation are truly staggering. There seems to be broad agreement that meetings are deeply problematic. The *New Yorker's* Cartoon Bank contains no shortage of cartoons that represent the meeting as an inept gathering, a troubling social form.

A range of one-liners also confirm this broad assessment. For example: "a camel is a horse assembled by a committee," or "a board is a group that takes minutes to waste hours." When I facilitate workshops on meetings, I routinely use the title, "Effective Meetings: How To Get as Little Done as You Do Now in Half the Time." This joke (which turns out to be approximately correct) is invariably greeted by knowing laughter. Managers spend a lot of time in meetings, whether one on one, in small groups, or in events or conferences. We have every interest in having our time spent well and spent on the right thing. This chapter aims to set you on the course to reclaiming some of that lost time.

LESSONS FROM MEETING MASTERS

In chapter 3, I discussed the process of "harvesting" and implementing best practices. In this chapter, I present the best practices of "meeting masters," dozens of individuals I have interviewed who run meetings right. Some I discovered; others were referred to me in a rolling, or snowball-type, sample. These women and men, hailing from organizations that span sector and size, facilitate meetings in remarkably similar ways. The difference from an "ordinary" meeting is palpable. Five elements stand out:

- The process is smooth and run well (efficiency).
- Action happens.

- Decisions get made.
- Decisions are of high quality (effectiveness).
- Participants have fun (authentic exchange, not a "fake" meeting).

These meetings provide a sense of accomplishment for the participants, something so rare that most of us cherish the opportunity when it arises. Attendance is remarkably high.

I have distilled these people's experience into a recipe, which I share in the following pages. It really works, but you have to actually do it. Like diet and exercise, knowing what to do is an essential first step; doing it is the second step. The recipe consists of *principles,* or general perspectives, and *rules,* the actual things you need to do. As you read, you will notice that meeting masters think about meetings differently from most. Rather than "having" a meeting, they consider themselves as "producing" a meeting (as in a play) or "giving" a meeting (as in a party.)

The Orchestra Principle

A meeting works best if you run it like an orchestral performance. A performance represents the *end* of a development process. The meeting should also represent the end of a process rather than the beginning. Orchestras have scores, which outline what will be played; meetings should have agendas. Orchestras have the appropriate musicians present; meetings should also have the appropriate players present. Members of the orchestra have been properly informed and trained prior to performance. Key players in your meeting also should have opportunity to prepare.

Purpose Principle

In good meetings, three things happen: you announce things, decide things, and brainstorm things. Only the last two must occur to necessitate a meeting. Do not have a meeting unless you need to decide or brainstorm. If you do not have things to decide or brainstorm about, then do not have a meeting. Many meetings are "newsletter" meetings and could easily be canceled or condensed into a memo. Others are "inform the boss" meetings. (The weekly meeting is often this latter variety.) Eliminate meetings like this.

Three Characters Principle

Most meetings are driven by the characters (people) in attendance. Meeting masters organize their meetings by the character of the items. They begin with a few announcements, then move to the decision items, and then, at the end of the meeting, brainstorm about upcoming items to get some ideas onto the table. Decision-making involves an intellectual process, which moves from many to few and then to one. Brainstorming involves going from one, to a few, to many. It is best to do the same type of intellectual work at the same time and not shift between the two. Decision-making must be done before brainstorming because decision-making breaks up group cohesion and causes people to become winners and losers. Brainstorming brings people back together and working toward the same goal. Brainstorming helps heal the emotional bruises that decision-making inflicts.

All meetings are divided into three parts. Meeting energy generally flows in thirds. The first third is called the "Get Go," which involves a few easy decision items and some announcements. The middle third is called the "Heavy Work," part and the last third is "Decompression." During compression (first third and second third of the meeting) people check out and drift away mentally. Brainstorming in the final third of the meeting re-engages participants. Brainstorming allows people to switch gears and start thinking a new way, which helps bring them back in. Brainstorming is fun and nonthreatening, and it gives people something new to focus on.

No More Reports/No New Business Principle

The masters have no reports during their meetings. People who gave reports were asked to break up their material into announcements, decisions, and brainstorming items. This allows the meeting to stay focused and not be derailed by new business. New business is what you assigned to be worked on at the last meeting. The manager acts as the agenda scheduler and requests that meeting participants submit these items ahead of time. The supervisor can then put each item in its appropriate place and get any additional resources to deal with an item.

The Business Process Principle

Masters view meetings as a business process, the output of which is a decision stream. In that perspective, the process can be examined, considered, and improved.

THE RULES

The rules are specific actions that the masters take to create a smooth flowing process. An excellent process does not assure an excellent result, any more than good ingredients and a well-equipped kitchen assures a good meal. But they are an excellent start to great results; without them, good results are often more random than realized.

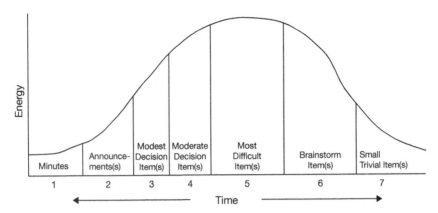

Figure 13.1 The agenda bell.

The Rule of 1/2

Masters receive all proposed agenda items halfway between meetings. That way they can compose the agenda, get the necessary information and people to the meeting in question, and start participants thinking about what they need from the meeting itself.

The Rule of 1/6

Masters structure the agenda so that about 1/6 of the material was from the past, 4/6 from the here and now, and 1/6 from the future. They invite forward-thinking and creativity at every meeting.

The Rule of 3/4

At about 3/4 of the way between meetings, the masters sent out the material. As one meeting master said, "giving people material at the meeting is like giving a musician a score and saying 'play this'; it is sight-reading and generally useless." The masters instead proposed a deal: I send the stuff out; you read it; we will get to it. They became like the professors for whom you always prepared.

The Agenda Bell Rule

The Agenda Bell (Figure 13.1) suggests that meetings begin with minutes, followed by announcements, some easy decision-making items, then the harder decision items, and then the most difficult decision items. The most difficult item is always located in the middle of the meeting where the greatest resources of attendance and energy are concentrated. If anything is going to break up the cohesion of the group, it will be in the middle. Hence, brainstorming follows that and the meeting sort of winds down (or more often, "whines" down) to trivial items like adjournment or items for an upcoming meeting. This style may take a while to get people into, but once they do, it can be self-reinforcing and enjoyable.

The Agenda Rule

The best agendas are designed like a restaurant menu. Each decision is, like each dish, separately listed. Underneath each decision is a little phrase of explanation and the name of the person who is going to handle it. To the right is a running clock. Time units are used to signal the flow of the process. An agenda with no times is like a menu with no ingredients. (See Table 13.1.)

The Rule of Minutes

Minutes are taken for substance, not as a court report. Each item on the agenda has its own paragraph. The substance of the discussion is reported, usually in passive voice. (The mileage allowance was discussed. Some were in favor of x, others favored y, etc.) Then a line is skipped and the decision or action is placed in a box for easy reference:

> The group decided to review what other agencies are providing for their mileage. John will report back next week.

CONCLUSION

The innovative meeting structure explored in this chapter creates a practical, achievable scaffold for the work of meetings: achieving high-quality decisions. It is to this competency that we turn in the next chapter.

REFLECTION

1. Select one meeting in your organization to use as a case study.
2. See what you can recall about the following:
   - How were preparatory materials distributed?
   - How were agenda items gathered?
   - How were items arranged on the agenda?
   - Were there any "newsletter" items on the agenda?

Table 13.1. An Agenda-Bell Meeting Agenda

Item	Content	Time	Notes
1	Minutes	2:00–2:05	
2	Announcements *New desks ordered*	2:05–2:10	
3	Retreat location *Key West seems best.* *ACTION	2:10–2:15	
4a	Vendor selection *A new software vendor wants to* *make a presentation.* *ACTION	2:15–2:25	
4b	Medical coverage *Should we extend medical coverage* *to all committed partnerships.* *ACTION	2:25–2:35	
5	Dress code *Should we retain casual Friday;* *go casual all week; or return to* *professional dress all week.* *ACTION	2:35–3:00	
6	Annual community appreciation event *Ideas for an exciting, different way* *to show stakeholders we appreciate* *their support.* *BRAINSTORMING	3:00–3:38	
7	Adjournment	3:38–3:40	

- How did the meeting handle time (start on time, end on time, cover all items in time allotted)?
- Who facilitated or led the meeting?
- How did this person help the meeting group navigate conflict and re-establish social cohesion?
- Did any distractions (food spills, phone calls, tech snafus, location confusion, etc.) impede progress?
- Now reflect on reasons why the difficulties might exist in your team's meeting.

- What, if any, incremental step could you suggest or implement that might begin improving your organization's meeting efficiency and effectiveness?

FURTHER READING

Tropman, J. (2017). *Team impact.* San Diego, CA: Cognella Press.

14

Building Effective Decisions

INTRODUCTION

Implementing an effective meeting structure that focuses on decision-making is not helpful if the decision-making process is not understood and managed. Good decisions are the foundation of any organization. Unfortunately, we all make bad ones—whether as individuals, groups, communities, organizations, or societies. There is no surefire way to avoid bad decisions, but in this chapter we explore techniques that help us make good ones in meetings.

Decision-making is a dynamic process, like the actual orchestra performance or the actual cooking of a meal. Once things are in play, they are, well, in play. Decision-makers need to think on their feet, go with the flow, go against the flow, know when to hold 'em and when to fold 'em. Meeting masters understand the deep structure of the decision-making process, integrate both the intellectual and interpersonal elements of decision-making, and manage both streams toward an intellectually robust and interpersonally acceptable solution. The likelihood of this happening without thought and attention is essentially nil. In fact, so common are rotten decisions that an entire genre of management literature explores them. To get a sense of what a good decision is, we'll dip our toe into the dark side of decision-making and look at some categories of really awful decisions.

ROTTEN DECISIONS: A BANQUET OF CHOICE

Decisions are designed to achieve results. Sometimes the results are above our expectations, sometimes they meet our expectations, and sometimes they fall below our expectations. For most decisions, the result or outcome is made up of the decision (the decision to marry, for example) and the implementation (making marriage work on a day-to-day basis). It is very possible, and we need to recognize this at the outset, that great decisions can be implemented in poor ways; it is also possible that poor decisions (you two are just not right for each other) can be made to work through creative and sustained attention to the issues of implementation.

(Some unlikely couples cultivate very successful relationships.) We might phrase the equation as:

Results = Decisions + Implementation

But we cannot rule out the role of contingency, or luck, in outcomes. Hence, a more complete equation might be:

Results + Decisions + Implementation +/- luck

Our focus here is on the "decision" variable. What are some classic types of bad decisions?

Folly

There are two versions of *folly*. One version was developed by historian Barbara Tuchman (1984) in *The March of Folly*. According to Tuchman, folly is a really bad decision, chosen from alternatives available at the time, and made by a group, not an individual. In his classic, "On the Folly of Rewarding A While Hoping for B," Steven Kerr (1975) frames folly as a situation in which one makes a decision for A and hopes it will result in B while actually focusing on A. This happens when people have a fascination with objective criterion, an overemphasis on highly visible behaviors, particularly face time, hypocrisy (lying), and a failure to emphasize outcomes rather than outputs. Each of these should be familiar to supervisors as this is especially important to them. It is important for the supervisor to actually try to understand the work that employees do and get into the depth of that work rather than stay at the surface of "objective" criteria, with an overemphasis on visible behaviors and a constant reporting of activities rather than results. Many organizations reward output measures, rather than outcomes. For example, employees are "rewarded for face time," being seen at the work site, rather than for the work they actually do. (For additional analysis of decisions characterized by folly see Elliot Cohen and John Gooch's [1990] *Military Misfortunes* and H. R. McMaster's [1997] *Dereliction of Duty*.)

Group Think

There are two versions of this flawed decision (Janis, 1983). The first is the "don't break the peace" version, found in very cohesive teams. No one in these teams wants to provide bad news. The team members sort of agree with everyone else until something catastrophic happens to break up the team. The other version, known as "capitulate to power," applies when a powerful administrator makes a suggestion that everyone publicly agrees with but privately disagrees with. In this situation people often hesitate to speak up and voice concerns and issues because of the power dynamic. They may at a later time fail to support the decision, speak against it, or otherwise sabotage the decision process.

The Abilene Paradox

A sort of management parable, the Abilene Paradox turns the spotlight on the leadership of agreement (Harvey, 1974). It is a story about a family living outside Abilene, Texas, that drove into town for lunch, with no air conditioning in the car, in 120° heat; as it turns out, no one actually wanted to go! We see this often when everyone does something that no one wants to do but everyone thinks that everyone else wants to do it because the decision options have not been articulated so that everyone actually knows that it *is* a decision.

The Garbage Can Model of Organizational Choice

Cohen, March, and Olson (1972) proposed that all organizations have four kinds of people:

- *Problem knowers*
  Know the problems that are being faced by the organization.
- *Problem solvers*
  Solve the problems the organization faces but might not know the problems because they are elsewhere.
- *Resource controllers*
  Control the allocation of money and other resources to a problem.
- *Decision-makers*
  Have the authority to put it all together and act.

Cohen et al. argue that most organizations assemble these people randomly as if tossed into a garbage can. Seldom do managers who construct a decision-making meeting agenda ask themselves, "Do we have the people in this room who know the problems? Do we have people who can solve the problems? Do we have the relevant resource controllers? Do we have the relevant decision-makers?" Often one of those groups is missing, and the team has to meet again: This is *rework*, and it costs organizations a lot of money.

The Boiled Frog

Tichy and Devanna (1986) report that, if you put a frog into cold water and very slowly heat the water, the frog won't notice because it is a cold-blooded animal. The frog will eventually boil to death. If you put a frog in boiling water, it will jump right out. Change has this effect on humans and organizations as well: It slowly works its way around us, and it may not be noticeably different enough for us to take action. Suddenly we are dead. So we have to pay attention to when we act and act proactively rather than waiting for external pressures.

The organization's rate of change has to be slightly greater than the rate of change outside your organization or it will die. Likewise, your personal rate of change must be slightly ahead of the organizational curve, or you'll find yourself professionally sidelined.

Defensive Routine

A defensive routine occurs in organizations, or families for that matter, and will be familiar to managers and staff alike (Arygris, 1985). A topic is undiscussable. This is common, for example, in families where substance abuse is an issue. For example, "We will not discuss Dad's drinking." Moreover, the undiscussability of this topic is undiscussable, so we will not discuss why we are not discussing Dad's drinking. We avoid any number of organizational topics: differential rates of compensation, the fact that Sally always comes in late, the boss's three changes in strategic plan within one fiscal year. And we won't discuss why we are not discussing those issues. These issues tend to fester until the organization faces a cataclysmic event and all hell breaks loose.

MANAGING THE DECISION

Decisions, like most things, go better if you follow well-established best practices rather than approaching them haphazardly. Structured approaches to decision-making can be helpful. The leader needs to help the group manage one step at a time, in the same order, and distinguishing between each step. Janis and Mann (1977) pioneered a set of steps that are still widely used:

- *Need*
  What is the problem or issue? What do we need to do?
- *Alternatives*
  What are the alternatives available, or that could be available?
- *Evidence*
  What does the evidence show? What can we determine about what the evidence proves?
- *Gains/Losses*
  How does this affect us? others? What are the pros and cons?
- *Commit to act*
  Use this information to make a decision.
- *Implement*
  Carry out the decision.

As time goes on, the decision-making group will become familiar with this liturgy and the benefits of following it. The group itself will enforce its application.

DECISION RULES: THE DEEPER STRUCTURE
OF DECISION-MAKING

The step-by-step approach is enhanced if you have a more thorough understanding of the dynamics of the decision process, each aspect of which needs to be managed.

- Decision rules
- Dominant elements
- Decision mosaic
- Rounds of discussion
- Decision crystallization
- Decision sculpting

Managing Decision Rules

A few guidelines (I call them rules), gleaned from meeting masters' experiences, can inform and guide the decision-making process and increase the likelihood of a high-quality decision. Decision rules are norms that make decisions okay. Managers must be aware that each of the five rules is at play in all decision-making settings even though some settings might emphasize some rules over others. The rule or rules that are most used in an organization (or family) is called a *decision culture*.

Consensus occurs when an option meets and can be shown to mesh with the decision culture. Managers must build a decision in a way that encompasses as many rules as possible. (See later discussion of decision crystallization.) They are usually used together because each rule advantages a subset of the group and disadvantages others. Hence, the five taken together provide a score of ongoing process of correction.

- *The Extensive Rule*
  The extensive rule takes into account what most people want. It is aimed toward creating the greatest number of participants and stakeholders. The drawback to this rule is that it always disadvantages the minority.
- *The Intensive Rule*
  The intensive rule counteracts drawbacks to the first rule by going with what makes people feel strongly: How strongly do they feel, and can we accommodate them?
- *The Involvement Rule*
  The involvement rule gives power to the people who have to carry out the decision, asks what they want, and asks how they feel about the decision options.
- *The Expert Rule*

The expert rule takes into account what the experts have to say; this includes scientists, lawyers, and those with experience. Experts are not always 100% correct, but they do bring valuable insight and expertise to the table.

- *The Power Rule*
  The power rule takes into account what the people with formal power in the decision-making group want, or what powerful external stakeholders want.
- *The Stakeholders Not in the Room Rule*
  This rule takes account of interests that are important but not present in the room.
- *The Other Elements Rule*
  Occam's Razor. Is it too costly? Is it too complex? Are there too many balls in the air?

This rule addresses other elements that may impact the decision: It might be too complicated, cost too much, or require staff we do not have. This rule enables components of a decision-making team to address problematic properties within a proposal or a decision option. Chief financial officers, for example, may identify issues with budget or revenue. Brand officers might notice a conflict with established communications priorities. Occam's Razor comes into play here: Generally speaking, the proposal with the fewest steps, the decision presenting the fewest complexities, is going to be a winning decision.

It is important to note that decision culture varies by group. That is, the prominent or predominant rules used to make decisions shift by organization or type of organization. In the military, for example, the extensive rule carries little weight. In Quaker, or Friends organizations, the intensive rule is highly important. Organizations can also have dominant and subdominant cultures. Decision-making often begins with the dominant cultures' preferences. A high-performing team will often assign, whether formally or informally, percentage weights for rules as they applied to their team. Successful decision maestros use these rules to crystallize decision options and transform them into decisions.

Managing the Dominant Elements

As with a jigsaw puzzle, there are better and worse ways to start managing a decision. With most puzzles you start with the corner and edge pieces. These might be called the dominant elements. Decisions have dominant elements as well. For example, consider a simple decision, "What shall we have for dinner tonight?" It is important to consider all the small parts of a decision and then start the discussion with the dominant element. This is the element that will most likely affect all other elements. Consider elements A through D. Element A affects B, C, and D; B affects C and D but not A. If you start with C, when you get around to A you will likely need to rework C and D because of the effects of A and B. That is *rework* in the decision process, and it costs a lot of time and money.

So start with A. Unfortunately, elements do not come with labels attached. There is no automatic way to identify A, so you have to identify the various elements and then come as close as possible to ranking them correctly. In the dinner example, a good candidate for A is "dine in or eat out." It will affect all subsequent decisions and, in this case, the very decision path along which you travel. If the answer is "out," then you begin to think of places to eat. If the answer is "in," then you begin to think of what is in the fridge. Starting with A helps to avoid rework and saves your organization time and money. (See discussion of the Guttman scale.)

Decision-Making as Mosaic Managing

Decision is really a collective noun. What we call a decision is usually a collection of small decisions assembled (not made) into a larger package. You "build" a menu made up of several small decisions. What should we have for dinner? Peas or beans; chicken or fish; rice or pasta; chocolate cake or strawberry pie? The mosaic of elements comes together and forms a larger decision. Understanding that decision-making is a process of putting together a puzzle is essential.

Manage Rounds of Discussion

A round of discussion occurs when everyone in a group has made one contribution to the discussion. At that point, in almost every group, there will be a slight pause in participation. At this crucial moment, the facilitator can intervene and speed up the meeting process. (It should, though, be a designated leader that moves the group to the next stage.) If intervention is not forthcoming, groups tend to continue recursive, unnecessary, and sometimes harmful, hashing over the same issue. Discussions are like freeways: when you see your exit, you have to take it or else you will just keep driving.

The decision maestro can sense when a group may need to go to a second or third or fourth round of discussion. But as that happens, the leader must ask that the next round *add to* the considerations, not *repeat* points from previous rounds of discussion.

Manage Decision Crystallization

Decision crystallization involves several steps. First, the facilitator summarizes what has been said during the round of discussion. He or she might use language like, "What I heard was XYZ." This is a neutral summary, which organizes and reflects to participants what they suggested.

The next step, which flows from the summary, is *vocalization,* a suggestion for action that the group can take. But simply presenting the action is not enough. That action needs to be legitimized; the group has to hear why it is okay. At this point we return to the decision rules to justify the action step.

A decision manager's script may often run something like: "What I hear from the discussion is (main alternatives). It seems, therefore, that a good possibility might be (vocalize a suggested action) because it appeals to most people (extensive rule), addresses the needs of the minority (intensive rule), is acceptable to the implementation team (involvement rule), and aligns with expert advice (expert rule), and the boss will sign off on it (power rule)."

At that point, the group will almost always assent. This process can happen at random, but it works really well if you follow the protocol suggested here.

Decision Sculpting

After the mosaic of small decisions has been assembled, piece by piece, into a larger decision, you can step back to see what pieces might need adjustment in order to improve the quality of the entire decision. This is best achieved later in the decision-making process, after you have a sense of all the elements involved, have ordered them to avoid rework, and have worked extensively with the decision-making team. For example, rather than considering simply whether to include almonds in the pilaf, you take into account the entire meal. When you do, you see that three courses already contain nuts; thus omitting the almonds might, in this case, result in a less repetitive and potentially conflicting profile. Similarly, as you look over all the elements of a decision puzzle, you may find that you will need to make some adjustments to the decision elements that comprise it.

CONCLUSION

Decisions are the lifeblood of organizational jobs, tasks, and work. Everything we do depends upon decisions, big and small. It is odd, therefore, that managers do not think more about what the decision-making process involves and what practices and procedures would improve it. This chapter contains two sets of suggestions. The first simply argues that if you use a predictable process, outcomes will be improved. The second posits a deeper structure to decision-making than most managers consider. Mastering this structure enables you to build complex decisions from bundles of simpler decisions through rounds of discussion. At the end of each round (when everyone has said one thing or all those who want to say something have spoken once), the facilitator crystallizes the decision by offering summative reflection followed by a suggested action that he or she legitimizes using the five decision rules. Legitimacy harmonizes conflicting norms (breadth of preference, depth of preference, involvement, expertise, and power) and fosters consensus.

REFLECTION

- Identify several decisions made within your organization (or your team) recently. What process was used to arrive at the decisions?
- Can you observe the "decision rules" at work in your organization's decision-making process? Which is dominant in your decision-making culture?
- Is your organization's decision-making track record characterized by any of the flawed decision categories? If so, which one(s), and why?
- Does your personal (or family, or community) approach to decision-making mirror or diverge from the approach taken by your organization? How are they similar? different?

FURTHER READING

Argyris, C. (1985). *Strategy, change and defensive routines.* New York, NY: Pitman.

Cohen, M., March, J., & Olsen, J. (1972). A garbage can model of organizational choice. *Administrative Science Quarterly, 17,* 1–25.

Janis, I., & Mann, L. (1977). *Decision making: A psychological analysis of conflict, choice, and commitment.* New York, NY: Free Press.

15

Writing Effective
Managerial Documents

INTRODUCTION

Although the format and structure vary by organizational sector, size, and funding mechanism, much of a manager's responsibility involves writing for a variety of audiences—requests for proposals, analyses, reports, memos, proposals, issue briefs, letters, policy statements, and press releases, to name but a few.

It is in the written document, usually, that the manager's many areas of responsibility are synthesized and his or her own perspective woven in. Documents are public and cannot be unseen, and interpretation of the author's intention frequently occurs without opportunity for the author to clarify. The ideas must be clear and organized by the time they are finalized in a written document.

To achieve these aims, managers need to anticipate a range of audience questions in written documents. They also need to take into account how their use of language structures and privileges alternatives, facilitates or hinders consideration, and makes processing ideas a winsome or painful undertaking. Since policy is simply the writing of ideas, the language in which those ideas are expressed can make all the difference, especially if some of the ideas are new. Writing is also the way in which thought is organized and finalized.

As with many management and leadership competencies, it is beyond the scope of this chapter to comprehensively address every aspect of effective writing. Instead, in the pages that follow I share the KnOWER system, an omnibus approach to organizing writing (Tropman, 1984).

REPORTS: THE KNOWER SYSTEM

Managers write all the time. The best managers know that writing is a process: There is rough carpentry and finish carpentry involved. Generally, writing works better if you identify a desired outcome and develop an outline that allows you to play with the ideas (sequence, order, and impact) without the pressure of simultaneously developing elegant prose. Once you have an outcome and a set of ideas, you can fill in the text. The KnOWER system, which I developed to organize my own writing endeavors, can help.

KnOWER stands for *Know, Organize, Write, Evaluate,* and *Rewrite.* Each phase is one component of the process. If the production of a draft can be viewed as a process, then the writer can have some sense of what a finished product looks like and what it will take for him or her to get there. As you become adept at such production, you will modify the system and develop your own. Too much detail is as harmful as too little, and the approach will not work well if you apply it in a heavy-handed fashion. Study the template, and then adapt it as appropriate to your own written work.

Knowledge (Kn)

Good writing begins when you have something to say, and an audience that needs to hear it. So first, identify your aim. Do you want to send a memo encouraging the use of a new technology? Second, find out a little about your audience. Writing is, after all, marketing. It is important to know who will be getting the message you need to give.

In suggesting this, I am not indicating that each writing project needs to involve a full-fledged opposition research project. For simpler projects, a few minutes of focused reflection will serve the purpose. What are the preferences of the demographic you are addressing? What kind of argument will the audience best respond to? Working with a university audience requires a more formal, scientific, well-documented approach. A business audience requires less documentation and more active prose. Board reports and executive communications should be simple and short.

After you identify your topic and get to know your audience, look at what is already known about your topic. The ability to find out "what is hot and what is not" is nonnegotiable. No one will read your memo if the airwaves are already saturated with written documentation, YouTube tutorials, and Tumblr feeds discussing the same point.

If you are writing about an issue on which opinion is varied, or divided, make an effort to mention, if not all, at least the primary views of crucial issues. Writers who hold a strong opinion may inadvertently (or intentionally) overemphasize their perspective while minimizing or excluding from the conversation those perspectives that differ from their own. This can lead to both a compressed conversation and, if a decision is at stake, a falsely limited decision. It can also lead to intellectual laziness: Opposing views are difficult to think about, so you avoid considering them. Take, for example, the issue of differences (or not) between male and female middle managers. There are opinions on the "differences" side and the "no differences" side. When the evidence is conflicting, it is fine to draw your own conclusion from that evidence. You must first meet two conditions: Present the two or more sides and explain the basis or bases for your advocacy. "My own experience suggests" is a fine basis, as long as you articulate it. As you write, be sure to record your sources. You may need them later, and others may ask for them. If you say "Research shows . . . ," you better have that research handy.

Organization (O)

Organization is the rough carpentry of writing. In most cases, thinking and writing are two different steps. Thinking is developing and organizing the ideas; writing is communicating them. As tempting as it is to open a Word document and dump all the things in your head (and as helpful as it can be to brainstorm like this), discipline yourself to do the thinking first.

Thinking first will take different forms, depending on who your audience is, what your purpose is, and what kind of document you're writing. Communicators have often likened thinking and organizing to construction projects. Like researching the site, drawing plans, and obtaining permits precedes construction, so the basic goals and audience analysis described previously precede actual drafting. Like excavating the site, pouring the foundation, and roughing in the frame precede mechanical and finish work, so determining your argument and approach, gathering your evidence, and putting it in order precede work on sentence structure, word choice, and typos. There are numerous good to excellent resources online for such "construction projects," none better, possibly, than Purdue University's Online Writing Lab (OWL).

These preliminary thoughts have historically been organized in an outline, although more recent concepts such as mind-mapping are also in broad use. An outline, or mind map, is a way of looking at the logical flow of your ideas without being concerned about how elegant your prose is. When you outline, you can more easily see the flow of the argument and the steps through which you want to take the reader, without too many words. It is sort of like what my grade school art teacher said: "When you draw a tree start without the leaves. That way the structure of the branches is clear. After you get that framed, then you can add leaves." Words are like leaves. The outline need not be detailed, though it can be, but the main points need to be there. Organize the evidence, then go to the next step.

Write (W)

Once you have the outline down, expand your ideas so that they are in prose format. Write quickly. Do not censor yourself; save that for the evaluation/revision step. You do not have anything to evaluate if you do not have anything on the page! If you're writing a short document, set a time goal, such as one hour for a draft of a letter or a two-page memo. (Remember, you've done the research and the thinking in previous phases. This is just transforming your ideas into prose.) For longer documents set yourself a page/time schedule, such as three pages a day. By the end of the week you will have a draft of 15 pages.

Evaluate (E)

Evaluation is a two-part process. First, look the document over and your own changes. But wait at least 24 hours before you do. Your brain needs time to reboot between creating the first draft and revisiting it.

Second, solicit reactions from others. This is both an intellectual and a political process. On the intellectual side, give copies (not of every document but of important documents) to those whom you believe can evaluate the strength of your argument and presentation and give constructive feedback. Remember that it is not necessary to follow every suggestion, but it is good to get a variety of perspectives. It is also important never to argue with or dissent from this kind of feedback. Ask recipients for insight and accept the feedback as just that, not as something you must implement. If you argue with responders, they will back away from responding (the asker is too high maintenance) and simply tell you it is great. Thus the value of feedback is lost. From a political perspective, it is wise to share your draft with "important" people or "opinion leaders." It is vital to know what parts may be politically sensitive and what words might be seen as outrageous. In each case, thank your reviewers at the time they give you the feedback and in documents where acknowledgement is appropriate. Sometimes you can work their comments and suggestions in as quotes or personal communications. Your draft is strengthened if you use the words and authority of others as well as your own.

Rewrite (R)

After you have reviewed the feedback, spend some time thinking about what you want to include and what not. Then prepare a second draft. Important documents often go through three drafts or more, so plan your research, organizing, writing, evaluating, and rewriting time accordingly. Otherwise, plan on working late.

CONCLUSION

The KnOWER system is designed to help managers be more effective in communicating ideas in writing. Keep in mind that the goal of writing well is not literary; it is practical. Your aim is clarity of thought, ease of comprehension, and audience-appropriate format and tone. These goals also hold true with verbal communication, to which we turn in the next chapter. (For the original, and much longer, version of the KnOWER system, see my *Policy Management and Leadership and the Human Services* [1984].)

REFLECTION

- What role does written communication play in your organization? (e.g., it's our primary product, so everything has to be perfect; we write down all of our policies and procedures and refer to them all the time; we are a digital office and communicate via Slack or Google chat—it's all shorthand and usually very practical; my boss uses email and text to send passive-aggressive threats; there are two of us in the organization, and we don't write anything down).
- How seriously do people inside and outside of your organization take the written documents you produce?
- How do you plan, organize, and execute research and writing assignments?
- Whose business writing do you admire and/or emulate? Why?

FURTHER READING

Davidson, W. (2015). *Business writing: What works, what won't.* New York, NY: St. Martin's Griffin.

Flesch, R. (1996). *The classic guide to better writing.* New York, NY: Collins Reference.

Tropman, J. (1984). *Policy management and leadership and the human services.* New York, NY: Columbia University Press.

16

Effective Verbal Communication

INTRODUCTION

Your staff, peers, and superiors need to understand what you are saying, and what you mean by what you say. The Three Penguins story illustrates the problems that can occur when communication goes awry.

A man is driving down the road and he sees three penguins along the roadside. He stops, picks them up, and puts them in his car. As he pulls into a gas station, the attendant observes, "You have three penguins in your car. You should take them to the zoo."

"You are so right," says the driver, and off he goes. About a week later the gas station attendant is out and notices the same car from a week ago, with the same penguins in the back seat, wearing sunglasses.

"Aren't you the guy I saw last week?" asks the attendant.

"I am," says the driver.

The attendant says, "I thought you were going to take those penguins to the zoo."

"I did," the driver replies. "We had a great time. This week we are going to the beach!"

This little story illustrates the perils of communication in management and leadership. The more important question, perhaps, is how to get it right, or at least better. For purposes of managerial communication, I want to touch on three areas: intrapersonal, interpersonal, and transpersonal (phoning and speaking), with the proviso that my insight is designed to give you an overview, a springboard for learning and developing your own expertise. My selection is again based upon talking with and observing managers over the years and coming to understand that there are a few simple things that we can all do to improve our communication.

BEGIN WITH THE AUDIENCE

The common theme throughout communication is *audience*. All communication has an audience, whether the person you are communicating with is yourself, others, or a larger group. All communication begins with the target. What is it that you want that audience to comprehend? In social work we have a phrase, "start where the client is," which applies exceptionally well to communication. Start with the audience. It is useful to repeat Steven Covey's injunction, "seek first to understand, then be understood" (Covey, 1990). At first glance it seems that Covey has it backwards: The key element in managerial communication is to be understood. But Covey realizes that if a manager or leader does not understand the audience and the audience's perspective, then communication cannot be tailored to be effective.

INTRAPERSONAL

Intrapersonal conversations are conversations you have with yourself. In fact, you are the person with whom you talk the most. This internal language and dialogue can contain negative self-talk and negative constructs. Negative self-talk usually sounds like a more sophisticated variation of, "I can't" or "I'm dumb" or "I'm failing." These thoughts can impact our interaction with others and erode a manager's ability to provide support to those they supervise. On this issue, Daniel J. Siegel and Tina Payne Bryson's (2018) *The Yes Brain,* while aimed primarily at parents, offers particularly helpful insights regarding the power of, and ways to manage, internal dialogue.

Negative constructs can be something like, "this problem, system, task, etc . . . is dumb." We observe negative constructs frequently as our children learn new skills. For example, two parents are watching their kids try to tie their shoes. One kid is not getting it and is crying in frustration, "this shoe is dumb." The other parent asks, "Why don't you help him?" The crying child's parent replies, "I am helping him." "This shoe is dumb" is an expression of frustration. We carry a little bit of that kid in us into our professional lives, and we have to watch for those problems of frustration to emerge. Negative internal conversations can inhibit organizational change, as individuals complain or blame rather than constructively plan.

We also need to silence our inner critic. Negative self-talk can initiate and support negative circularity and a downward spiral or self-esteem. Instead of giving in to these negative internal thoughts, managers can and should cultivate positive reflections that reflect their strengths. We need to do this regularly because in a high-pressure job, problems sometimes seem greater than our strengths.

Much of our internal conversation reinforces our assumptions. We think we "hold" assumptions, but often, in reality, our assumptions "hold" us. When we think of ourselves as choosing the assumptions we hold, we can also recognize the possibility of changing those assumptions. That's the danger of bad assumptions and that is why we need to scrutinize them carefully. Supervisors' assumptions about workers and their work need constant reexamination and reflection. As sociologists William Thomas and Dorothy Thomas (1928) observe, "Things thought to be real are often real in their consequences."

THE PROFILES AT A GLANCE

WHAT's YOUR STYLE?

Check off the traits that generally apply (keeping in mind that you probably behave differently in different groups and situations). Tally up the relevant traits in each category for a rough gauge of which styles you draw on most often.

☐ Outgoing	☐ Diplomatic	☐ Quantitative	☐ Methodical
☐ Focused on the big picture	☐ Empathic	☐ Logical	☐ Reserved
☐ Spontaneous	☐ Traditional	☐ Focused	☐ Detail-oriented
☐ Drawn to risk	☐ Relationship-oriented	☐ Competitive	☐ Practical
☐ Adaptable	☐ Intrinsically motivated	☐ Experimental	☐ Structured
☐ Imaginative	☐ Nonconfrontational	☐ Deeply curious	☐ Loyal

HOW CAN YOU GET THE MOST OUT OF EACH STYLE ON YOUR TEAM?

Know what gets them excited—and what they find off-putting.

ENERGIZED BY:

Brainstorming	Collaboration	Solving problems	Organization
Spontaneity and trying new things	Communication	Directness	Predictability and consistency
Enthusiasm	Trust and respect	Winning	A detailed plan

ALIENATED BY:

Rules and structure	Politics	Indecision	Disorder
The word "no"	Conflict	Inefficiency	Time pressure
A focus on process	Inflexibility	Lack of focus	Ambiguity and uncertainty

Figure 16.1 The profiles at a glance.

INTERPERSONAL

Managers also need *interpersonal* communication skills, a competency comprised of several more discrete practices.

Communication Style

Managers need to understand their own style of communication and its implications. Very much like understanding your temperament (see chapter 7), it is very helpful to assess your communication style.

As with temperament, it is useful to think of these as describing your default style, not as defining you. Douglas (1998) suggests four basic styles: Director,

Table 16.1. Douglas' Basic Communication Styles

Director	Expresser
Talks in action verbs	Speaks rapidly
Cares about the bottom line	Uses animating gestures
Always on the go	Entertaining
Speaks crisply	Thinks out loud
Talks about goals	Talks about ideas
May seem insensitive	May be imprecise
Thinker	**Harmonizer**
Talks about details	Talks about people
Inquiring	Sensitive to others
Often makes lists	Avoids conflict
Speaks carefully	Dedicated and loyal
Wants things done "right"	Speaks softly
May procrastinate	May overcommit

Source: Eric Douglas (1998). *Straight talk: Turning communication upside down for strategic results at work* (Palo Alto, CA: Davies-Black).

Thinker, Expresser, and Harmonizer. According to Douglas, these styles reflect a range of personality traits that comprise a communication style, and each style tends to favor two of the four.

As a manager, it is not only useful for you to be familiar with your own style but also the personal communication styles and preferences of each staff member. If Douglas, for example, is right, as you complete his assay two of these will immediately seem "right" to you. The other two will seem less close and comfortable. When you have completed the self-analysis, seek to understand the styles of others. When you start with the audience in mind, appeal to them not as much through your style (although there will always be some of that) but through theirs.

Gender and Communication Style

Linguist Deborah Tannen (1990), conducted groundbreaking studies in gendered communication styles and gendered communication styles in professional settings. Although not all adhere to gender-unique communications styles, her points are useful to keep in mind. In particular, she suggests that the fundamental purposes of communication may be different. Men, she suggests, engage in "report talk," which involves directing and conveying information, as reflected in the use of slide decks, newsprint, and so on. Connection with the audience is secondary. Women, on the other hand, engage in "rapport talk," the primary purpose of which is to establish connection; the conveyance of information tends to be secondary. Although the divisions are less stark than they may have been as society is more fluid and managers and leaders place more emphasis on communication, the implications of gendered communications still influence daily professional interactions.

Avoiding Communication Traps

Managerial communication, especially with staff and peers, can entrap the manager in surprising ways. Among these is the "monkey-on-my-back" phenomenon, which occurs when a staff member complains about something he or she cannot do. The manager, especially in a community benefit organization, may try to be helpful by assisting in, and sometimes taking over, the entire task. Rather than responding to a complaint immediately, train your staff in "creative complaining": anytime someone comes to you with a problem, he or she also has to have at least one solution to the problem. Thus, the conversation focuses on the solution, not the problem.

Blame and Credit

Managerial conversations involve giving credit and assigning blame, a responsibility that can be strengthened by using the "mirror and window" approach. As humans, we have a tendency to look in the mirror when credit is to be assigned and out the window when blame and responsibility is to be distributed. The opposite is a better practice. When problems arise it is better to look into the mirror rather than out the window. Looking in the mirror requires us to first assess our own contribution to the problem and *then* look out the window at the contribution of others. For every finger of blame pointed at someone else, three fingers are pointed back at you.

There is a tendency, however, to avoid blame and seize credit. That is why supervisors have a supervisor, managers sometimes do, and executives rarely do: it is hard to request supervision when it's not mandated. Hence, as one moves up the organizational ladder, it is wise to continue to have a "supervisor" or mentor or coach with whom you review your work and behavior.

Praise in Public, Blame in Private

The setting in which blame and credit are delivered makes a huge difference in how well they are received. Praise in public. It gives staff the encouragement to continue with their work and also lets them know they are doing the job correctly. Managers and leaders who practice giving praise publicly know that they get more leverage from a good comment not only with the intended recipient but also his or her team. Effective managers offer criticism privately, to avoid shaming staff in front of peers or other supervisors and causing them to feel as though they must defend themselves to the group. While this point is obvious to most, a significant number of managers feel that public humiliation is a good motivator (it is, but it motivates only hate and sabotage). Moreover, managers of this ilk avoid praising in public because they believe—whether implicitly or explicitly—that it detracts from their reputations.

Feedback

We all need both positive and negative feedback about our work. Positive feedback helps us to know that we are moving in the right direction. Negative feedback offers guidance about how to improve. Despite this, some employees may experience a fear of feedback of any sort. Part of this fear may not come so much from the feedback itself but from the clumsy and random way that it is delivered. If feedback is not skillfully delivered, valuable information is lost, because awkward transmission of information provokes uncomfortable emotions, causing staff to avoid or ignore the information. Moreover, if feedback is infrequently delivered—for example, if you document all assessment of staff activity but only share it in a formal performance evaluation—your staff has no opportunity to reinforce praiseworthy behavior or alter the trajectory of damaging behavior.

Most importantly, positive and negative feedback need to be delivered in the context of an authentic relationship. If you have not cultivated trust over time, a staff member will look askance at any input you offer—whether laudatory or corrective.

Negative Feedback

Effectively given, negative feedback probably is *the* best performance improver. Feedback differs from criticism and should focus on the problem rather than the person. Effective feedback is a nonjudgmental and nonfateful observation about how anyone (staff, peers, or bosses) can improve performance. Feedback should be problem oriented, connected to the topic, and close in time to the event. The person providing the feedback should be able to accept his or her part of the problematic situation. Moreover, managers and leaders must also "own" their feedback and not refuse to accept responsibility for it. For example, saying to a staff member, "I wanted to give you a raise but (insert other party here) would not let me," if it is not 100% the case is, in fact, a lie. Your staff will know, whether intuitively or via informal information channels, that you are lying and that you lack the courage and confidence to speak with integrity.

Manager/leaders should avoid giving direct advice and use phrases like "Perhaps, . . .," "Something that has worked in similar situations . . . ," or "You might consider . . . " that allow the employee to "choose" the suggestions, rather than being ordered to do it. Another way to open a conversation in which you intend to give negative feedback is to ask your staff member about his or her motives and/or thought process. This alone will help you better understand the circumstance and tailor your feedback appropriately. Always check for comprehension prior to ending the conversation.

Make sure that you distinguish feedback conversations from those of a "disciplinary" nature, among them coaching and counseling.

Coaching and Counseling

Whetten and Cameron (2015) highlight the difference between *coaching*, the clarification of information, and *counseling*, which is appropriate when a staff member's attitude interrupts the flow of work.

Managers and leaders coach when they pass along information, give advice, set performance standards, and/or help staff to improve. Problems with coaching arise when a supervisor lacks sufficient information about a circumstance, does not fully understand the nature of the problem, or is not letting the worker practice the coaching suggestions before evaluating. Supervisors' responses during these times are direct. They must advise, reorganize, and provide suggestions.

Counseling, as Whetten and Cameron use the term, is not analogous to therapy. Rather it is a sympathetic conversation during which the supervisor or manager seeks to understand, and help the staff person understand, the blockage and how to overcome it. In a sense, it is the emotional work of supervision. Unlike coaching conversations, counseling conversations are nondirective. The supervisor must probe for information, reflect upon what the employee communicates, validate the employee's affect, and ask for answers. In these interactions, employees may appear defensive and project their difficulties on others. They also may have difficulty recognizing the nature of the problem and may not be show much willingness to change. Counseling problems stem from fear of fault, blame, failure, and success. Some problems can however be simply attributed to temperament clashes. The intervention that a "shooting-star" staff member requires is one example of a counseling conversation. The steps advised there—careful documentation, preparation, and specific benchmarks within a specific time frame—are essential protocols to follow when counseling a staff member.

These conversations can be unnerving, particularly for a young manager, since they involve confrontation and conflict. However, it is possible to minimize, and even move beyond, this discomfort by determining in advance what the goal of the conversation is, framing the conversation as not personal, viewing it as encouraging the mission of the organization, role-playing the conversation in advance, and engaging in basic mindfulness practices that reduce natural fight-flight-or-freeze responses to conflict.

TRANSPERSONAL COMMUNICATION

Some communication is *transpersonal*: People are involved, but they do not communicate face to face. Most commonly, these include telephone conversations, messaging (whether email, text, Slack, Twitter, or other instant messaging programs), and presentations. Given the ubiquity of transpersonal communication, as well as time zones involved, digital offices and remote organizations, organizational managers are almost always on call 24/7.

In some positions, and in some industries, this is essential. But it poses at least two problems. First, it reduces your margin and can increase your Index of Difference (see Table 7.1, "Managing Yourself"). If you are at a family event but you are texting with staff about the content of tomorrow's press release, you are working for your organization while you are attempting to be present with your family. Sometimes this is unavoidable, but it should always be undertaken mindfully. Second, transpersonal communication can limit the amount of information your staff receives, whether they only hear your voice on the telephone or only read your words via email, text, or a 140-character tweet. This limitation can exacerbate uncertainty and can leave room for interpretation (or misinterpretation) of your message or guidance. While a number of managerial matters can be effectively handled with the economy and dispatch of electronic communication, matters of importance, those that are nuanced, and those that are emotionally charged are best managed in person. Not only is the full range of communicative channels available, making it is easier to check for understanding, offer clarification, and receive feedback, but it avoids potentially truncating the thought process—a temptation with abbreviated modes or limited channels of communication.

Telephone

Managers often overlook telephone communication because it is ubiquitous. Yet it needs to be considered. The phone is, well, the phone. But remember that tone of voice, sense of friendliness, pace, and cadence are as important or more important because the added channel of nonverbal communication is missing. Moreover, talking directly to a person can sometimes improve the efficiency of routine communication such as appointment setting. The arrangements can be made in one quick, focused effort rather than in an inefficient exchange of seven or eight texts or emails detailing—for example—where, when, and length of appointment.

If you have trouble getting people to take your calls, it may be because they recognize that you are a "high maintenance" caller—you take a long time to get to the point, you only call when you need something, and so on. Naturally, folks would not want to answer the phone, let alone call you in the first place.

Telephone Skills

1. Prepare
   A call is like a meeting. Take time to prepare both your thoughts and emotions. Jot your main points; take a few minutes to clear your mind. If the call is complex, send an agenda in advance.

2. Establish time parameters

   Ensure your available time is understood by your conversation partner in advance of the call. Schedule conversation items so that you can complete them in the time you have available. As in a meeting, begin with easy items, place the tough ones in the middle, and end with brainstorming (see chapter 13).

3. Conclude

   Very much like guests who are loathe to leave a party, some calling partners will linger. It is important, therefore, to alert partners when you have only about five minutes left to talk. If necessary, use some of that time to schedule another call.

4. Follow up

   Once the call is complete, make notes and send them to the calling partners with appropriate follow-up information.

5. Manage your anger

   Given the complex and shifting nature of managerial work within formal organizations, the difficulty of harmonizing systems, the delicate balance of product and process, and the failures and flaws that will undoubtedly emerge, encountering and experiencing anger is inevitable. Depending on temperament, preferred communication style, and position in the organization, many of us pick up the phone and call when we are angry. This is not a good idea. We are less clear and cogent when we are angry, and our anger brings out defensive anger in others. Neither is it good to write when angry. A better plan is to wait a period of time and explore what means of communication would be most productive for the long-term good of the project or organization.

6. Manage others' anger

   As a recipient of an angry call, try not to enter the dance of anger. Simply accept what the caller is saying as information, not agreement. Take a deep breath—or 10—and exhale slowly to calm the automatic adrenaline dump that inevitably accompanies a perceived threat. It is often possible to apologize without compromising your position or your organization, even if something is not your fault—regretting the unfortunate occurrence without accepting a damning assessment of your personhood or worth. If possible, schedule a follow-up conversation to address any actual issues that fall within your purview, or route the caller to the appropriate party to address a real or perceived cause for anger. Check in with yourself and your stress level afterward (see chapter 7; as a manager and leader on whom others depend, caring for yourself is paramount).

MAKING PRESENTATIONS

Presentations involve speaking to, rather than with, groups of people—a different type of interaction than occurs in a meeting or discussion group. Presentations vary so widely, in fact, that I'll avoid giving you specific advice and instead share a few insights that you can adapt to your own circumstance, style, and responsibility.

1. *Watch the clock*
   Presenters say too much and talk too long. Less is almost always more. Practice your presentation, since it is often difficult to tell how long it actually takes until you run through it.
2. *Speak from an outline*
   A word-for-word text begs you to read it, word for word. When you look up from a text, it is difficult to find your place again. If you fumble, you will lose your audience. The solution? Use an outline and practice speaking in advance so that you know what you're going to say.
3. *Prepare your outline in larger font*
   Use 14 or 16 point. It is much easier to find your place as you're glancing up at your audience and back to the screen or page—even if you have young eyes!
4. *Make copies available*
   Provide copies for the audience to follow along with you. Include your name and contact information so people can follow up after your talk.
5. *Use PowerPoint (or KeyNote, or Prezi)*
   PowerPoint or another presentation program can be a lifesaver for your presentation. If used well, it integrates your spoken remarks and with visual engagement. But failing to follow basic design principles can make your PowerPoint presentation a punishment for your audience—possibly even worse than a poorly run meeting.
6. *Employ appropriate humor*
   If you tell a joke or share an anecdote, be sure that it's snappy, to the point, and relevant. Ensure that it doesn't consume an inappropriate proportion of the remarks. (See recommendation 1. A few practice run-throughs will set you apart from the rank amateurs.)
7. *Foster participation*
   Whenever possible, foster audience participation in your presentation. For example, invite people in groups or at tables to spend a few minutes in semi-structured, open-ended conversation about your material. Then invite some to share insights with the audience.

8. *Use game films*

   Watch and listen to recordings of your presentations. It may be painful,
   but—especially if you're working with a coach or colleague—you will get
   a good sense of negative mannerisms and ineffective practices and will
   be able to replace them with more effective tactics.

CONCLUSION

Effective verbal communication is an ongoing process of achieving mutual understanding. Understanding does not mean, nor does it require, agreement.
Achieving agreement is a separate process. You can't achieve authentic agreement
with peers or bosses, and you can't expect your staff to perform efficiently and effectively, if you don't share a clear grasp of the issues at hand.

There are a range of factors to consider. Begin by understanding your audience.
Get a feel for the group or person to whom your message is directed. What are
their preferred styles of communication? What is yours? How are you communicating with yourself about the topic at hand? Reflect on the medium of communication. Do you have the luxury of an in-person conversation, or are you limited
to a call, text, or email? These and other factors—implicit and explicit—will shape
your experience. But you can't go wrong by beginning with Covey's dictum, "Seek
first to understand, then be understood" (Covey, 1990).

REFLECTION

- What are the primary methods and uses of verbal communication
  in your organization's culture—both internal to the organization and
  external to stakeholders, community members, and vendors?
- How effective (doing the right thing) and efficient (doing it the right
  way) is verbal communication, on the whole?
- In which areas would you judge yourself to be most competent? least?
  Why and how?
- How often do you achieve your aim during the first round of verbal
  communication? What factors contribute to, or detract from, this?
- In an anonymous upward review, how would your staff respond to this
  question?

FURTHER READING

Gallo, C. (2014). *Talk Like Ted: The 9 public-speaking secrets of the world's top minds.*
   New York, NY: St. Martin's Press.
Huber, A. (2018). *Telling the design story: Effective and engaging communication.*
   New York, NY: Routledge.
Kehoe, D. (n.d.). Effective communication skills. *The Great Courses.* www.thegreatcourses.
   com

PART 6

The Executive Edge

Honing and Sharpening

For all administrators, from those beginning supervisory and managerial work to those in C-level positions, regular refreshing and periodic retooling are key elements in ensuring a sharp personal and organizational edge, or continuous improvement in performance. For convenience, I borrow the terms *honing* and *sharpening* from the cutlery industry. In this section, we explore ways to cultivate and maintain a sharp, well-balanced edge for both you and your organization.

While both honing and sharpening are necessary for maintaining an edge, they are not identical. To understand the distinction, we first need to know why knives become dull. When a knife dulls, the sharp edge has been lost and/or the blade's edge is no longer aligned properly due to use. So, even if the blade is sharp, losing alignment means that it won't cut through food properly. Alignment and edge are restored through the processes of honing and sharpening.

HONING

A honing steel pushes the edge of the knife back to the center and straightens it. It corrects the edge without shaving off much, if any, of the blade's material. Honing doesn't actually sharpen the knife. But if honed properly, the knife will seem sharper because the blade has returned to the proper position. Honing should be done often: Some even hone before each use. For executives, using oneself in so many ways on a daily basis creates problems in alignment. For executives, regular coaching sessions are the "steel" that helps maintain alignment and edge.

SHARPENING

Unlike honing, sharpening is a process that grinds and shaves off bits of the blade to produce a new, sharp edge. It can be done using a water stone, whetstone, or electric knife sharpener. Sharpening can be done less frequently than honing—just a few times a year depending on how much use the knife gets. For the executive, time out of the office for a development event is the equivalent of sharpening.

17

Keeping Your Executive Edge

In this chapter I touch on leadership perspectives, leadership activities, and phases of leadership growth that will help you develop and maintain your edge.

EXECUTIVE LEADERSHIP PERSPECTIVES

An executive leader must, above all, be competent—knowledgeable and skillful in execution. Successful chefs and maestros are models of competence: Not only do they know their respective fields, but they must implement—or lead others in implementing—a range of tasks with seamless precision. The chef is consistently responsible for designing the menu, assembling the ingredients and staff, and executing the meal. Maestros consistently research and select programs, rehearse and prepare orchestras, and conduct performances. A range of competencies enable the executive leader to succeed, a few of which we discuss here.

Know the Difference Between Management and Leadership

Management and leadership are distinct but essential in an organization. We introduced this concept with the double helix in the introduction to part 1 of this volume. Here, though, we expand on a few of the ways in which this difference works out in formal organizations. In each case, the work of managers and leaders is symbiotic and supports the health, growth, and mission of the organization.

POSITION VERSUS ROLES
Management is a position, from beginning manager to the CEO. Leadership, however, can be practiced from any position. And it can, and should, go beyond the workplace to include home, community, state, and nation. Consider it an "every way/every day" activity.

Tactics Versus Strategy

To adopt a military metaphor, management is tactics. It focuses on *how* to achieve the goals of the organization. Leadership is strategy. It focuses on what the goals are and why they are important in the broader environment. In the military, you'll often find that the quartermaster (responsible for ensuring that the troops are fed and supplied) is a manager. Similarly, you'll find that the brigadier general (responsible for identifying direction and conceptualizing campaigns) is a leader. Nautically speaking, management is driving the ship and leadership is plotting the course.

Visioning Versus Organizing

A leader sees and communicates possibilities—a new population to serve, product to offer, or strategic partnership to pursue. A manager harmonizes systems within the organization and organizes the execution of the leader's vision.

Select the Right Tool and Avoid Overuse

How do you know which skill set to access? That is, how do you know whether a circumstance, an initiative, or a problem requires a leadership approach or a management approach? Some instances are obviously one or the other. But in many cases it is not as clear whether one is more helpful than another. A general rule I have found helpful is to select the opposite of what is going well at the moment. If the organization (or yourself) is well managed, then some leadership initiatives (visioning, strategizing for the future, posing disruptive questions) might be good to try. If the organization (or you) has a lot of ideas and initiatives but nothing seems to be crystallizing, then some emphasis on management (regulating, organizing, setting up procedures) might be the way to go.

Many of us are better in one area than the other. It is all too often the case that individuals tend to fall back on the approach that comes more naturally and to ignore the less comfortable approach. This is the "When you are a hammer, everything is a nail" phenomenon. It leads to wooden performance rather than nimble application. A related danger here is the "strengths perspective," which argues that you should strengthen your strengths and outsource your weaker areas. There is some wisdom in that. But you still have to select the right tool and use it, even if you have to outsource it because you do not have it.

Constant Review

In chapter 3, I discussed the after-action review and lessons-learned document that is standard practice in the U.S. Army. Most managers and leaders, in my experience, skip the lessons learned. If the event or activity succeeds, there is a feel-good period accompanied by a pat on the back. But there is no review. If the event or activity fails, there is a feel-bad period, comprised of offloading responsibility (blaming others, the weather, etc.) and still, no review. Review and harvesting—even if you're busy capitalizing on your success, or even if you're embarrassed by your failure—are essential components of growth for managers and leaders, the organizations they steward, and the populations they serve.

LEADERSHIP ACTIVITIES

Practice Contributory Leadership

Contributory leadership involves being proactive rather than standing by. A contributory leader is one who chips in rather than cops out, one who leads from the ranks. He or she embraces a "let's do it" attitude rather than a "not right now" approach. You'll know contributory leaders by observing who steps up to fill a gap or solve a problem by suggesting solutions, proposing a course of action, or asking solution-oriented questions. These leaders help out where they can, when they can, in the ways that they can—with a focus on cultivating the greater good.

Practice Servant Leadership

Servant leadership is a state of mind. The manager and leader sees him- or herself as a helper, facilitator, and coach, rather than as the boss. They are focused on achieving organizational goals by supporting the organization from a motivational and practical perspective. You will know them by their after-you (rather than me-first) orientation to work, success, and recognition. These are the leaders who "look out the window rather than in the mirror."

Practice Everyday Leadership

When leadership is integrated in work and professional life, it becomes an everyday habit. Everyday leaders lead irrespective of position or sector. You'll find them exercising leadership at home, in the neighborhood, at school, in community settings, and wherever the opportunity presents itself. It's simply what they do.

PHASES OF LEADERSHIP GROWTH

Develop a Plan for Self-Improvement

Staying sharp and honed requires a commitment to learning, improving, and growing. And it is a real commitment, because, as managers and leaders, your time is at an absolute premium. Without this commitment, you'll find yourself sequestered in a silo—in your own practices, organizational culture, and

LEVELS OF COMPETENCE

We evaluate executives on their mastery of eight leadership competencies (listed in the far left column), assessing where they fall on a spectrum from 1 (baseline) to 7 (extraordinary). We have found that four traits–curiosity, insight, engagement, and determination–predict how far managers will progress. Below each competency are the traits linked to strength in it.

	1	2	3	4	5	6	7
RESULT ORIENTATION PREDICTED BY • DETERMINATION • CURIOSITY	Completes assignments	Works to make things better	Achieves goals	Exceeds goals	Improves firm's practices and performance	Redesigns practices for breakthrough results	Transforms business model
STRATEGIC ORIENTATION PREDICTED BY • INSIGHT • CURIOSITY	Understands immediate issues	Defines plan within larger strategy	Sets multiyear priorities	Defines multiyear strategy for own area	Changes business strategy in multiple areas	Creates high-impact corporate strategy	Develops breakthrough corporate strategy
COLLABORATION AND INFLUENCE PREDICTED BY • ENGAGEMENT • DETERMINATION • CURIOSITY	Responds to requests	Supports colleagues	Actively engages with colleagues	Motivates others to work with self	Facilitates cross-group collaboration	Establishes collaborative culture	Forges transformational partnerships
TEAM LEADERSHIP PREDICTED BY • ENGAGEMENT • CURIOSITY	Directs work	Explains what to do and why	Gets input from team	Inspires team commitment	Empowers teams to work independently	Motivates diverse teams to perform	Builds high-performance culture
DEVELOPING ORGANIZATIONAL CAPABILITIES PREDICTED BY • ENGAGEMENT • INSIGHT • CURIOSITY	Supports development efforts	Encourages others to develop	Actively supports team members' growth	Systematically builds team's capability	Aids development outside team	Builds organizational capability	Instills culture focused on talent management
CHANGE LEADERSHIP PREDICTED BY • ENGAGEMENT • DETERMINATION • INSIGHT • CURIOSITY	Accepts change	Support change	Points out need for change	Makes compelling case for change	Mobilizes others to initiate change	Drives firmwide momentum for change	Embeds culture of change
MARKET UNDERSTANDING PREDICTED BY • INSIGHT • CURIOSITY	Knows immediate context	Knows general marketplace basics	Investigates market and customer dynamics	Deeply understands market	Generates insights about market's future	Identifies emerging business opportunities	Sees how to transform industry
INCLUSIVENESS PREDICTED BY • ENGAGEMENT • INSIGHT • CURIOSITY	Accepts different views	Understands diverse views	Integrates other points of view	Functions well across diverse groups	Facilitates engagement between factions	Strategically increases employee diversity	Creates inclusive culture

SOURCE EGON ZEHNDER

Figure 17.1 Levels of Competence. Used by Permission from Harvard University Press.

limitations. So, whether you default to management or leadership approaches, set learning goals in both areas. You'll need to plan for two off-site educational/ professional development events each year. Plan to include some costs in your personal budget. Generally, community benefit organizations do not have a continuous learning culture; their budgets for this kind of investment are limited because they do not prioritize it. To ensure that your personal growth doesn't fall through the cracks, try the three-legged stool approach: You pay a third, your organization pays a third, and you and your boss (or your board, depending on your position) fundraise for the last third. And remember, your expenses are tax deductible as an unreimbursed employee expense. Much of this work can be folded into your professional routine, both independently and locally.

Set aside time to read. As with any educational undertaking, regularity is key, and a little each day will go a long way. As you read, look for managerial and leadership practices to learn from—to emulate or avoid. Skim at least three papers a day, one national, one local or regional, and one trade. Subscribe to professional journals that highlight cases of management and leadership such as *Harvard Business Review, Fast Company,* and *Stanford Social Innovation Review.* As discussed in chapter 7, get together with others to discuss what you're reading and engage a leadership/management coach. Consider keeping a leadership/management journal where you record interactions, observations, conundrums, successes.

Track Your Competence

There are myriad ways to assess your growth in executive leadership competencies over time. Not all need to be complex, time consuming, or expensive. For example, *Harvard Business Review* recently published an article that focuses on curiosity as a key leadership platform (Fernández-Aráoz, Roscoe, & Aramaki, 2018). Members of the Zehnder consulting firm, the authors lay out eight skill areas and seven growth phases (see Figure 17.1).The seven growth phases are very helpful. Numbers 1 to 3 are essentially management phases; 4 is a fulcrum point; and 5 to 8 are essentially leadership phases. The only drawback is that it is a lot of keep in mind. Had I been doing it, I would have had a three-sided triangle with one face having 1 to 3 (now labeled M1-3); the second face having 5 to 8 (now relabeled IL-3), and 4 on the third face (now labeled T—for Transition).

CONCLUSION

Maintaining your executive edge is essential to continued success in professional and personal life. It begins by developing the perspective of an executive and cultivating the range of competencies that enable you to go from good to great, and—once you get there—to continue growing. As both research and experience suggest, the two skillsets are not identical. In *What Got You Here Won't Get You There,* Goldsmith (2007) identifies a list of behaviors and habits that sabotage the successful executive (see Table 17.1).

Table 17.1. Twenty Habits That Hold You Back from the Top

1.	Winning too much	The need to win at all costs and in all situations—when it matters, when it doesn't, and when it's totally beside the point.
2.	Adding too much value	The overwhelming desire to add our two cents to every discussion.
3.	Passing judgment	The need to rate others and impose our standards on them.
4.	Making destructive comments	The needless sarcasms and cutting remarks that we think make us sound sharp and witty.
5.	Starting with "No," "But," or "However"	The overuse of these negative qualifiers that secretly say to everyone, "I'm right. You're wrong."
6.	Telling the world how smart we are	The need to show people we're smarter than they think we are.
7.	Speaking when angry	Using emotional volatility as a management tool.
8.	Negativity, or "Let me explain why that won't work"	The need to share our negative thoughts even when we weren't asked.
9.	Withholding information	The refusal to share information in order to maintain an advantage over others.
10.	Failing to give proper recognition	The inability to praise and reward.
11.	Claiming credit that we don't deserve	The most annoying way to overestimate our contribution to any success.
12.	Making excuses	The need to reposition our annoying behavior as a permanent fixture so people excuse us for it.
13.	Clinging to the past	The need to deflect blame away from ourselves and onto events and people from our past; a subset of blaming everyone else.
14.	Playing favorites	Failing to see that we are treating someone unfairly.
15.	Refusing to express regret	The inability to take responsibility for our actions, admit when we're wrong, or recognize how our actions affect others.

Table 17.1. Continued

16.	Not listening	The most passive-aggressive form of disrespect for colleagues.
17.	Failing to express gratitude	The most basic form of bad manners.
18.	Punishing the messenger	The misguided need to attack the innocent who are usually trying to help us.
19.	Passing the buck	The need to blame everyone but ourselves.
20.	An excessive need to be "me"	Exalting our faults as virtues simply because they're who we are.

A list of behaviors and habits that sabotage the successful executive, from In What Got You Here Won't Get You There, Goldsmith (2007).

These reflections are useful, but they are hard to implement independently. Thus, the final observation here is that meeting regularly with an executive coach (see chapter 7) will help you keep these suggestions and others in focus, help you to take them under regular review, and champion you as you strengthen the practice of them. Surgeon Atul Gawande (2011), for example, noticed that after several years in the operating room, his skills had reached apogee. He sensed that he was no longer improving. So he asked a former teacher to come observe him. Afterward, he was embarrassingly relieved to learn that the professor had a number of small suggestions that could help him improve. As Gawande explained, you don't need a coach because you are bad at what you do; you need a coach because you're good but you're plateauing.

REFLECTION

Often, we adopt practices and perspectives as we go along, without knowing that we have internalized them or what we need to do to keep them "cutting edge." This is often the case with leadership. Take a few moments to reflect on the leadership styles presented earlier in this chapter.

- Which of them describes your approach? What practices do you use to carry them out in a professional setting? a community context?
- Do you remember where or when you learned them, or whose example you modeled your leadership approach on?
- What other leadership KSAs would you like to add to your repertoire as you move along your career path? Where/when/with whom did you first encounter these?

- What trusted coach or mentor could evaluate your current practice and suggest ways to bring it to the next level?

FURTHER READING

Collins, J. (2005). *Good to great.* New York, NY: HarperBusiness.

Peters, T., & Waterman, R. (2006). *In search of excellence: Lessons from America's best-run companies.* New York, NY: HarperBusiness.

18

Succeeding While Leading

Achieving and Maintaining Balance

All supervisors, managers, and leaders—all of us—desire "success." It is "the American dream." Success is a premiere driver of the American psyche. It was what eluded Willy Lowman in *Death of a Salesmen*. None of us want to be the "low person " on the totem pole or on the bottom rung on the social ladder. We like our success big—the bigger the better. In the land of Big Macs, seven-figure bonuses, a 14,000-square-foot hideaway (for two), and Humvees, it is almost as if size really does matter. The focus on big and more begs the question of balance and proportion. My classes have interviewed "successful" executives for dozens of years. Many of these respondents regret their overemphasis on work. They lament their missed anniversaries, kids' birthdays, games, plays, and the like. The old Harry Chapin song, "The Cat's in the Cradle," speaks to the dad with no time but promising something later: "We'll get together then, you know we'll have a good time then."[1] Now in later midlife, these icons feel hollow and they sense that "real" success might have eluded them. Others feel that success is always ahead of them—whatever they achieve is tainted by their very possession of it. It is like the old line from Groucho Marx, "I don't care to belong to any club that will have me as a member." Among the many problems with "success" is the question: What *is* it, anyway? This chapter suggests that balance is the key to success and offers, as well, a tool to monitor your progress toward "it" and your drift away from "it."

If you look on Amazon.com you find over 17,000 listings for books on "success." (Google has 590 million!) There are thousands of quotes about success. Much of the thinking on success emphasizes the point I mentioned before—big, public recognition of some achievement or series of achievements. Certainly, if you have more than anyone of a desired good, you are a "success" in conventional terms. Many say that having "more" trumps failures.

But there is also the sense that too much of a good thing is, well, a bad thing. "Money is the root of all evil" (1 Timothy 6:10) is one popular example of "too

---

1. https://www.azlyrics.com/lyrics/harrychapin/catsinthecradle.html

much of muchness." Power, as well, is a problem in large amounts. "Power corrupts; absolute power corrupts absolutely," is a famous phrase from Lord Acton. We are also aware of people destroyed by status seeking, by desperate attempts to get the top job, and so on. It seems that success might be better seen as a balance among elements, rather than a huge amount of one element.

Based upon my interviews with lots of executives, I have provisionally concluded that there are five goal sectors that need to be balanced for a person to "feel" success.

There is no specific set of proportions for these five goals that are right for everyone. Each of us needs to work out an appropriate balance and rework that balance as our life changes. The one imperative is that you should not let any one goal area be less than 20% (Figure 18.1). This is most especially true in personal and X factors—they usually go first if pressures mount; family goes next. Apart from some minimum distribution, what is important is that you imagine an ideal distribution and then check it against what is "really going on."

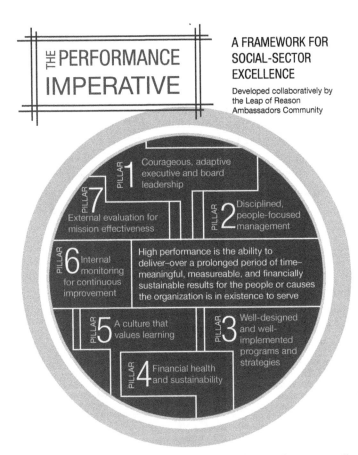

Figure 18.1 The performance imperative: A framework for social-sector excellence.

CONCLUSION

Success is something all managers crave, and I believe is in the grasp of many, if thought about correctly. Dying with the most toys is not, for most, a measure of success. However, if that floats your particular boat, knock yourself out! Most of the work I have done suggests that a managed balance leads to long term success in life, very much as it does in your financial portfolio.

As you move through your career, there will be changes in your balance. The "ideal" column will become reweighted. Pressures will cause you to discover "Allocations" in the "Real" column that you did not plan. You will need constant oversite and adjustments. But that's management and leadership.

Managing is, as Peter Vail (1989) said, a performing art. It is fun to bring people and resources together and produce outcomes, events, innovations, and results. Desirable conclusions (because results and outcomes can be bad, like decisions) do rarely happen by themselves. Guidance is essential for systems and/or agencies to function well and to continually improve that functioning. Management and leadership provides that guidance even though managers are unappreciated. Bad managers are usually noticed because employees flee them, results are poor, and they are continually off-loading responsibilities on "the system" or whatever. Good managers are the unsung heroes of the organizational enterprise.

As you can see, there is a lot to know to be a good administrator and the material here is just a start, but it is a good start. By the time you have mastered even some of this material, you will be so far ahead of your contemporaries that you will be promoted to a post of executive leadership. That is another challenge!

19

Conclusion: Hanging On or Moving On

The Perils and Promise of Executive Transition

We can do no better than to reflect on Ralph Waldo Emmerson's definition of success:

> What is success?
> To laugh often and much;
> to win the respect of intelligent people and the affection of children;
> to earn the appreciation of honest critics and endure the betrayal of false friends;
> to appreciate the beauty;
> to find the best in others;
> to leave the world a bit better, whether by a healthy child, a garden patch Or a redeemed social condition;
> to know even one life has breathed easier because you have lived.
> This is to have succeeded!
> — RALPH WALDO EMERSON

In some instances, the best way to keep yourself and your organization sharp is to transition out of your position. Sometimes it's easy to identify when this is the appropriate option. Sometimes it's very difficult. Regardless of whether the path is clear or muddled, transitions (and this holds true for any transition in life—not just the professional version) are complex. They are fraught with the tension of moving from one place to the next. At their best, they are exciting and difficult. At their worst, they are horrible and difficult. In this chapter we'll explore why executive transitions are particularly complicated.

The tension between hanging on and moving on occurs in all phases of life. Everyone is born, and everyone dies. (Some of us stick around for a long time.) Moving on from, or hanging on to, a destructive habit, such as substance abuse, is excruciating. Moving on from, or hanging to, old ideas and perspectives can be too. Take, for example, the Flat Earth Society (created by Samuel Shenton in 1956). And of course, any executive transition involves moving from one job to another, leaving the old job and its perks and comforts, and moving on to a new one with many unknowns.

EXECUTIVE TRANSITION

Executive transitions may be up or down or involve a lateral move to a different area. Such moves always have implications for the mover and for those around him or her, including family, friends, and work colleagues at the old location and new destination.

Executive transitions can be voluntary or mandatory. But like all transitions change is a process characterized by the well-known steps of *unfreezing, changing,* and *refreezing,* frequently attributed to Kurt Lewin (Business 101: Principles of Management, n.d.). The process is full of ambivalence. During *unfreezing,* a person begins to disengage or disassociate from the past. During *changing,* the person experiences confusion as he or she discerns and develops the skill sets and behavioral repertoire required in the new circumstance. During *freezing,* the person becomes accustomed to the new mindset and his or her comfort level returns.

During the transition process, some people leave the old while they are still there (anticipatory departure and socialization). Others go to the new and drag the old with them (the new job is just like the old one . . . only bigger).

HANGING ON

In the "hanging on" scenario, the executive leaves but actually stays. *Staying* can take several forms. Sometimes it is physical, as when the executive's new office is just down the hall from his or her replacement. Or sometimes the executive does not have another position (between jobs) and just hangs around his or her old place of employment, looking forlorn, to others if not to him- or herself.

Can't Let Go, Even Though They're Gone

Sometimes the transition is emotional. In this instance, the executive cannot leave the old relationships and perhaps the old perks, even though he or she has left the position. He or she may often try to act out through former staff and colleagues. This situation often includes an expectation of loyalty from former staff, who are themselves "moving on" in adapting to their new boss. Such emotional expectations create a stressful climate among the former staff members who are on the receiving end of such expectations.

False Promisers

Sometimes executives realize they should leave (retire, take a different position) but just cannot bring themselves to do it. So they promise that they are in the process of leaving—but this is a lie. And sometimes they actually believe the lie. Executives like this often say, "Yes, I will be moving on . . . Just not yet." Since they have "said it," colleagues are hesitant to reach out to them about specifics and the charade drags on. After a while the staff realizes that the boss is never going to leave. A number of developments occur at this point: The staff are angry at the boss and withdraw work support, angry at themselves for being duped, angry because they themselves now have to leave, and angrier still with the realization that they should have left long ago.

Lame Ducks

False promisers and executives who announce a retirement date well into the future become lame ducks. Immediately their power diminishes. Succession politics begins. Other members of the leadership team begin to ally themselves with likely internal and external successors. Initiatives stall or are dropped "until the dust settles." The organization goes into a "stall." Talented staff do not want to wait until "next year" when the supposed event will occur; they begin to look for other positions.

Founders Syndrome

Founders syndrome occurs when founders either remain too long in an executive position or, having relinquished that position, remain a "trustee for life." They become "enmeshed" in their "baby" and cannot let the organization move on.

LACK OF SUCCESSION PLANNING

Most organizations, it is fair to say, do not have a succession plan in place. Such lacunae tend to perpetuate the retention of the current CEO who is "not quite ready" to move on (or will never be ready). Lack of succession planning is similar, in many ways, to the avoidance many people practice regarding their wills and advance medical directives. Succession planning (of which a will is one personal example) involves recognizing that transitions are inevitable and that they require decisions about the future that create stress and discomfort. Avoidance and denial appear to be the easier course, if ultimately more problematic. Yet it is important to plan out how you will resign, what work you will complete, how you will leave that work to whomever will be taking over for you, and what you will tell people when they ask you why you are leaving. No matter what your experience in this executive position was like, you want to be remembered as someone who helped solve problems and was a team leader.

THE DEEPLY CLUELESS

Consultants suggest that half of the folks who think they are going in to meet with their boss for a promotion are actually going to be fired. They cannot read the signs of the times, so their transition is a shock. Transition shock adds another element to normal transition complexities. Some therapists call this a "narcissistic wound." Those who receive a narcissistic wound cannot unfreeze—sometimes for quite a while. As Bridges (2004) points out in *Transitions*, "one cannot move forward if one is chained to the past."

MOVING ON

Moving on is also rife with complexities. Unfreezing may be gradual, as with planned retirement. Or it may be sudden, as with a firing. In either case, departing executives often leave with a "golden parachute," which is designed to protect them from job loss and financial risk when a change of control, such as a merger or being fired, occurs. In the 1980s, when companies were frequently acquired in hostile takeovers, this was done to ensure that CEOs would negotiate good deals for their companies. Boards of directors offered generous severance packages in the event that the new owners dismissed the CEOs. The company and CEO agree to the terms of a golden parachute prior to the CEO's appointment, as part of the contract. Parachutes can be worth millions of dollars. Hewlett-Packard's Carly Fiorina received $40 million when she resigned after being asked to step down.

Regardless of whether the moving on is voluntary or mandatory, gradual or sudden, there are several patterns.

Leaving While Staying

In this scenario, the executive emotionally leaves the current job while still employed at the current job. Such executives have "moved on" before they leave. They tend to diminish their work effort (why bother?) and shift their investment to their next phase, real or imagined.

The Destructive Mover

Sometimes, new executives are smashers and slashers. This person takes a destructive approach, citing everything that the departed executive did as suspect and tarnished. Whatever the previous executive promoted, the new executive seeks to destroy. President Trump is the most public recent example of this type of "moving on." For such executives, everything must be their idea or creation. A new vocabulary that diminishes the work of their predesessors evolves. Rather than improve and enhance what their predecessors have done, they destroy it because of their own psychological needs.

Just Like My Old Job, Only Bigger

Frequently job-movers are not able to see that the new job is qualitatively different, not just bigger than, their old job. Hence, they apply the same wheelhouse and skill set to the new job and fail to unlearn (or bracket) some older skills while employing new ones. A perfect example of this is the CFO who becomes CEO. CFOs tend to see problems in financial terms; CEOs need to have that perspective, of course, but also embrace a significantly broader view. Some CFOs can make this transition; many cannot. Leaving one job for another job should be because you are making an upward career move—or a necessary lateral move—to give you the experience for the next upward move. Taking a new position to get out of your current one is just wheel-spinning. Whenever you leave one position for another, make sure you are taking that step to move toward something, not away from something else. I would also suggest that it is unwise to leave one position for another simply because of money. Rarely is money the reason a person likes his or her job.

The Player/Coach Dilemma

A slightly different version of the "old job" problem is the player-coach dilemma. Excellent players are often invited to be coaches. However, good playing and good coaching are very different skills, and really good players are frequently not very good as coaches. While this truism is not always the case, it stems from the observation that doing something well yourself, as your own product, is a skill set quite different from assisting a team to optimal performance.

SUCCESSFUL LEAVING AND MOVING ON: HELPING THE EMPEROR GET SOME NEW CLOTHES

Given these perils, how can success in both leaving and entering positions be improved? It is likely that executives—who, as a group, are not all that self-reflective since they tend to be action-oriented—may not be in the best position to recognize potentially toxic elements in their own mindset and behavior, both involving the departure mindset and their entering mindset. This is complicated by the fact that executives usually occupy important and powerful positions, and it is painful, and sometimes dangerous, to "speak truth to power." A decent solution for entering a new organization is to engage a coach for a while. Although some are not naturally coachable, it may be a starting place for many entering executives.

When is it time to leave? Data indicates that most CEOs start doing what they like to do, not what the organization needs them to do, after five years. Founder's syndrome is not unique to the founding board members. It can be detected in successful long-term executives as well. It is most likely time for the CEO not to continue "hanging on" when he or she is bored with the job, impatient with and irritated with the board and staff, resistant to change, disinterested in business travel, and downright tired and fatigued. You have achieved your goals and vision, and it is now time to "move on."

Finally, it is important to recognize that regular performance discussions by the board or senior executives should include some forward planning. As suggested before, many (the deeply clueless) just do not get the message that it is time to move on, or they get that message and reject it or fail to act on it (the false promisers).

CONCLUSION

In this chapter, we touched on Lewin's theory of the change process and surveyed a few of the patterns of change that executive transitions follow. While transitioning out of a leadership role may sharpen the organization's edge, it is a complex process for the departing executive.

REFLECTION

Whether professional or personal, change is—both practically and emotionally— a one step forward, two steps back process. Take a moment to reflect on your professional life or the life of your organization.

- At what junctures have you experienced major change? Do you anticipate a change in the near- or medium-term future?
- Examine one experience of change (or more if you're interested) and how the unfreezing-changing-refreezing process unfolded for you both practically and emotionally. Did the process follow a linear pattern (progress only in one direction), a recursive one (revisiting steps multiple times), or a different pattern altogether?
  Unfreezing: You disengage or disassociate from the past.

Changing: Confusion as you discern and develop the skill sets and
   behavioral repertoire required in the new circumstance.
Refreezing: You become accustomed to the new mindset and your
   comfort level returns.

FURTHER READING

Bridges, W., & Bridges, S. (2017). *Managing transitions: Making the most out of change,*
   (4th ed.). Boston, MA: Da Capo Lifelong Books.
Dotlich, D., Noel, J., & Walker, N. (2004). *Leadership passages: The personal and professional transitions that make or break a leader.* San Francisco, CA: Jossey-Bass.

Activities Activities connect events. They are the time period between the completion of one task bundle and the beginning of another task bundle.

After-action report Piloted by the U.S. military and now widely used in civilian sectors, an AAR is a systematic review of what happened in a project or assignment. Often consolidated into a lessons-learned document, as part of the harvesting process through which organizational learning occurs.

Assessment Planned review of progress against expectations. Usually done in thirds or quarters, over the time period of the project, so that there is time for "mid-course correction."

Autonomy constraint Micromanagement, overchecking, and anxious supervisory behavior convey to staff that they are incompetent or untrustworthy. When autonomy is constrained, whether explicitly or implicitly, workers feel, and are, devalued and undignified.

Boards of Trustees (also Boards of Directors) Serve as conservators of the organization and are tasked to provide policy direction and executive appraisal.

Budget The allocation of resources over the life of jobs, projects, and work. Money and time are the primary resources budgeted. Budgets provide controls and goals or targets toward which investments should be made.

Bundles The items you include in (or omit from) an "issue package." Bundles are assembled with consideration for who might sign on or off, depending upon what is in the issue package.

Career path A planned journey through a career, the career path concept is helpful for talking about progress and growth. The path may include stops within the current organization but usually involves moving on at some point.

Coaching Informational work of supervision. Manager/leaders coach when they pass along information, give advice, set standards of performance, and/or help staff to improve.

Community benefit organizations An umbrella term that encompasses nonprofits, public organizations working for community benefit, and for-profit organizations that include positive social impact in their mission.

Competence Competence encompasses the acquisition of knowledge and the development of skills in a particular area. Staff, managers, and executive leaders all move along a competence continuum—from novice to beginner, along the path to journey person, reaching the level of expert and then master—as they grow in a particular area. As people grow in competence, they grow in efficiency and effectiveness, learning to do the right things in the right way.

Conceptualization Ability to see the whole project in its entirety. When conceptualizing, a manager sees the parts, elements, events, and activities needed, as well as their sequences and interdependency.

Consultant Professional or firm that distills knowledge gleaned from advising a range of clients to advise and support future clients. Community benefit organizations most frequently engage evaluation consultants; investment in managerial and executive coaching and organizational development are less common.

Counseling The emotional work of supervision. Manager/leaders counsel when an employee's attitude interferes with work. Unlike coaching, these conversations are exploratory, not directional. But because they involve the management of emotions and negative performance, they require careful preparation by the manager.

Cross-cutting skills These are skills that are essential regardless of position on the organizational staircase.

Decision criteria Bases the manager/leader sets for her or his own decision-making and that of the organization.

Efficiency and effectiveness Efficiency means doing things right. Essentially, it means following the procedures and protocols for job performance. At minimum, efficiency means satisfactory performance. Managerial supervisors work toward producing optimal performance. Effectiveness means doing the right thing. You can be efficient doing incorrect or unnecessary tasks. Hence, the dual focus of the manager/leader is to do the right thing, the right way.

Effort ratio The weight or time emphasis that you expect to be allocated to the work and/or within which you expect the work to be done. A clear effort ratio answers the question, "How much of all your time should be spent on this aspect of the essential job?" Failure to articulate these weights leads to misunderstanding downstream.

Elements Aspects of a project that are ongoing and tend to occur throughout the process of the project.

Emotional intelligence Capacity to identify and channel your emotions as they arise. Comprised of self-awareness, feeling management/leadership, motivation, empathy, and social skills.

Emotional management/leadership Managers recognize that staff bring feelings to work and that "managing" feelings and emotions is a core part of management and leadership.

They recognize the emotionality of situations, respond appropriately to expressed feeling, encourage and channel appropriate feeling into constructive pathways, and navigate their own and others' emotions.

Evaluation The process of performance oversight and measurement. Following the establishment of front-end goals, oversight consists of periodic check-in meetings to monitor progress. Assessment is a mid-point meeting that judges overall progress. A final performance appraisal checks goal achievement and results in a grade. Early evaluation is heavily feedback centered. Later-stage evaluation grades whether staff work to (or above) standard, where the grader is more powerful than the "gradee." Finally, the evaluator translates evaluation research into actual changes in program practices.

Events Nodes in the project process, where one task bundle ends. Also termed milestone.

Executive Staff at the C-level—or top leadership team—of the organizational staircase. They balance internal oversight with external matters that affect the organization or that the organization wants to affect. They provide meaning and purpose to employees, clients, consumers, and customers of the organization. Executives initiate change from strength, not crises, and avoid causing crisis during change. They also supervise—administrative support staff, for example—and manage—chief of staff and their team, for example.

Executive transition Change in jobs, moving from one job to another. May be up or down, lateral, voluntary, or mandatory. Process of change characterized by excitement and ambivalence. Can be characterized by hanging on, not wanting to separate from the past. Can also be characterized by moving on or letting go.

Executive coach Experienced professional whom you pay to talk with regularly as part of your professional growth. He or she has more knowledge and experience than you, understands management issues and your industry and sector, and is able to serve as a resource. Distinct from a mentor, the coach will conduct an initial assay to understand your style and personality, guide you to essential reading and key conferences, and challenge you to further professional growth.

External network Those outside the organization with whom you connect with on a regular basis, who are outside the culture of your organization, and even outside the culture of your sector. It might include friends; priest, minister, imam, or rabbi; or others in whom you have confidence.

Feedback Feedback is nonjudgmental observation about how anyone (subordinates, peers, or bosses) can improve performance. Feedback should be problem oriented, connected to the topic, and close in time to the event. Feedback should be descriptive and validating, given often, and distinguished from "disciplinary" conversations. Provider of feedback must be able to own his or her share of responsibility for a problematic circumstance.

First-position management Managing with both authority and responsibility. Managers with authority may be anxious when managing subordinates because they feel completely responsible for everything the subordinate does. This anxiety creates a tendency to adopt the "Because I said so" or the "My way or the highway" options as core managerial styles.

Founder's syndrome Popular term for a difficulty faced by organizations where one or more founders maintain disproportionate power and influence following the effective initial establishment of the project, leading to a wide range of problems for both the organization and those involved in it.

Framing The case for stakeholders to get involved in (or refrain from getting involved in) an issue. Effective framing requires articulating both the business and cultural reasons that should guide involvement decisions. Effective framing also requires ample preparatory work.

Goals Goals are targets to work toward. There are generally five goal sectors, which need to be balanced for a person to "feel" success. These include: personal goals, partners and family member goals, work goals, civic goals, and X-factor goals.

Grading A qualitative, though evidence-based, judgment on how well staff performed in a specific, agreed upon ahead of time domain.

Growth Professionally, growth entails developing competence in a role, position, or skill set. "Opportunity for growth" is an important aspect of "soft" compensation as organizations become flatter, opportunity for advancement decreases, and employees seek portable knowledge that will benefit them during careers with varied organizations.

Guttmann scale Array of tasks, A through I, which has the property that A impacts B through I, B impacts C through I, but not A or B, and so on. This dominance hierarchy of tasks needs to be observed; otherwise the system will have significant rework.

Harmonizing systems Vital to good work and successful living regardless of system. For example, value systems in conflict, antique behavioral systems not attuned to best practices, tensions among and between project staff, conflicts over resources, conflicts among projects, or others.

Innovation Improving the procedures and processes you are already doing. Staff should consider it part of their job to innovate (to improve the job), and managers should consider encouraging and overseeing the outcome as part of theirs.

Inputs Materials the organization or program takes in and processes to produce the results desired by the organization. Inputs are often associated with a cost to obtain and use the item; budgets list inputs and the costs to obtain and/or use them.

Intersection of challenge and skill "The place of most potential" for each person. Operating at this intersection places them "in the flow." Managers promote this by understanding where each worker is and which tasks, at which levels, will help them cultivate a sense of flow. They increase workers' skill by adding appropriate increases in the level of task. It is maintained by increasing task complexity as skill levels increase.

Invention Adding products, services, treatments, or interventions that do not currently exist in your organization. Senior management and leadership must establish a process within the organization for selecting some inventions to pilot. A climate of supportive permission is needed to prevent the organization from becoming stuck in the mud.

Involvement The intensity and time point of "buy-in" from other stakeholders during the issue development process. Remember: Buy-in requires build-in; if stakeholders are involved at the front end, the back end is much more pleasant.

Job Your job description, or the job description of your staff. Perhaps better called a "job scaffolding," under which your job is constructed. Your first task in manager/leadership is to extract an "essential job" out of all the jobs, select the list, or package, to which you must attend (if managing yourself) or the package to which your direct report(s) should attend.

Leadership Capacity to motivate and inspire without force. It is a role you can fill regardless of position; you can lead whether you are a program assistant or a CEO. Leadership is possible in any context—family, neighborhood, agency, community, or nation.

Leader/manager The first managerial step on the organizational staircase. The core of the supervisory responsibility is ensuring the supervisee completes assignments that they fit into the job package appropriately. This bundle becomes more general at the project- and middle-manager levels. Managerial foci tend to be unique at each level, but some functions are similar regardless of level on the organizational staircase.

Logic model Typically depicts the inputs, processes, outputs, and outcomes associated with an organization and its programs. Communicates the logic behind a program, its rationale, the underlying "theory" or set of assumptions or hypotheses that program proponents have about why the program will work, or why it is a good solution to an identified problem.

Margin Financial stability and profit. In CBOs, mission drives margin, and margin acts as an important boundary. You do perform services not in your mission just because they have margin. Likewise, you do not offer services that fall within your mission because you have the margin to do so.

Means/ends chain Quality is essential in both job process (means) and outcome (ends). This dual focus is always important, because outcomes are nested in a means/ends chain. Managers must dip into that chain to ensure that means and ends are functioning and synchronous. Like other chains, this one is only as strong as its weakest link. The most vulnerable and critical areas of the chain need special attention.

Mentoring A professional relationship that focuses on employee growth. Both employee and mentor should be looking to the future, or the next level of the employee's career, laying out steps to achieve those targets. Mentors work with employees across the whole mentoring spectrum, from participating in organization-sponsored formal programs to creating informal relationships.

Micromanaging Too much checking or overfocus on dates and deliverables. Often is an indicator that the middle manager is not doing the motivational task. See also autonomy constraint.

Middle managers Responsible for meaning making; connecting the organization's mission to jobs, tasks, and work; ennobling the work of the organization; talking the organization up rather than down. They insist on quality work at all levels; attend to development, career pathing, and employee growth and encourage and support innovation and invention. Middle managers have more than one project or a much larger project for which they are responsible.

Mission Purpose or meaning that underlies the organization's work. All organizations have a mission, even if implicit. Meaningful work is of vital importance to staff and is created by managers, rather than inherent in the work itself.

Multitasking For administrators at any level, multitasking requires attending to both lower-order jobs and the three "umbrella" tasks of supervising, managing, and leading— shifting many times among levels and tasks each day.

Organization An entity that has identifiable structural and cultural features, one of the forms through which society organizes itself. All organizations have both formal and informal structures and task and process foci. However, their nature varies widely by mission, sector, size, and location in the growth cycle. Max Weber identified the following elements in an organization: Division of labor, Administrative apparatus, Hierarchy of authority, Impersonal rules, and Fulltime jobs/careers.

Outcomes The (hopefully positive) results of the organization's work. CBO outcomes are usually specified in terms of: learning (including enhancements to knowledge, understanding/perceptions/attitudes, and behaviors), skills (behaviors to accomplish results, or capabilities), and conditions (increased security, stability, pride, etc.).

Outputs Tangible results of organizational processes and activities, usually accounted for by their number and frequently misunderstood to indicate success of an organization or program.

Overwork Exploiting workers and getting them to work cheap or for free; extracting work from employees while denying them choice or compensation. This kind of overwork is prevalent in CBOs, sometimes disguised as "commitment," where going the extra mile is considered appropriate behavior.

Parts Temporally and functionally discrete jobs that are episodic. They start and finish at some point within the project process and accomplish some subgoal. They may reappear at intervals in the project.

Peer management Securing cooperation, follow-through, and execution from organizational peers over whom you have no direct authority. There are two groups of peers: First, those who have similar or identical positions (they are peers whether they are at the same organizational level or not) and second, everyone else in the organization. In all cases, attend to the quality of relationship and manage via positive connectivity so that, when you need their help, they will be happy to assist.

Performance appraisal Looks over the total performance of the worker for a year or any defined period of time. This process is distinct from, but related to, project appraisal, which is part of the overall performance appraisal.

Periderailment Predisposing/antecedent behavioral styles that lead to derailment include organizational, interpersonal, and intrapersonal elements. Organizational elements include: failure to build a team and delegate, failure to think strategically, overreliance on a narrow circle of advisors, and failure to know the business and deliver positive results. Interpersonal elements include an abrasive style, which alienates employees and halts information sharing. Intrapersonal elements include low emotional intelligence and failure to manage emotions.

PERT and the Critical Path PERT (Program Analysis and Review Technique) is a method for charting events and activities for a project. An event has a beginning point and an ending point. An activity is the path, or the time between events. Each activity has two time estimates attached to it. t^e is the expected time to complete the activity. t^m of

t^l is the maximum time available. When $t^e = t^l$, this is the "no slack path" The alert manager will coach workers to leave extra time in the path so that there is wiggle room in case Murphy's Law decides to spring into action. The no slack path is one kind of critical path. The other is the longest path; it tends to dominate the planning process.

Prioritization Understanding your ideal time distribution and the actual time distribution you have achieved or defaulted to.

Product The actual outcome the organization seeks to deliver. The outcome is the result of jobs, tasks, and projects coming together regularly over time. Product production must be seamless, regular, dependable, and accountable.

Project Interrelated set of tasks that exist over time and are designed to accomplish a goal within an organization. A project is comprised of assignment bundles. The bundles need to be formed into coherent batches. These batches, in turn, are sequenced appropriately so that the desired outcome (deliverable) can be achieved by the desired time (date). Project refers to the whole package of task bundles. May be an ongoing organizational function or a one-time event. Usually a team of employees is assigned to complete the project.

Project Aristotle A Google study of the characteristics of successful and less successful teams in its organization. The most successful teams included: psychological safety, dependability, structure and clarity, meaning of work, and impact of work.

Project manager Responsible for a particular product or event. Manages a budget of money, people; supplies, and expectations. Completion of the project involves sequencing or linking jobs and tasks and supervising one or more direct reports (or people assigned to work on that project). Project completion within time and budget is the central goal, and the employees' work (or that portion of the employees' work you supervise) is aimed at accomplishing that project within temporal, legal, and financial constraints.

Project Oxygen A Google study of the question "What is an excellent manager?" The research team identified eight managerial imperatives drawn from the personal skills of their best managers.

PSOSBPE Supervisors, managers, executives, and leaders at all levels use a toolkit commonly created out of the following elements: Planning, Strategizing, Organizing, Staffing, Budgeting, Programming, Evaluating. These are the essential tools of the administrative trade and are used throughout an administrative career, albeit at increasing levels of generality as one ascends the managerial staircase.

Psychic income and impaired dignity What happens at work is of great importance to us as people. Of central concern is our meaning and dignity, or psychic income. Having a meaningful job is one part of psychic income. The other is being treated well at and by work.

Resilience Capacity to bounce back from stress and overcome obstacles. In emotional intelligence literature, it is part of what is called "optimism."

Reward systems How the organization "pays" for employees' commitment and performance. In addition to monetary and fringe benefit compensation, reward systems involve the opportunity for professional development and growth and the opportunity to do meaningful work in a place where one is appreciated.

Schedule control Schedule control in projects involves three basic skills: conceptualizing the project, realistically estimating the time each component will require, and communicating both the components and time to the organization.

Second-position management and leadership In conventional understandings of management and leadership, you manage from the second position when you have responsibility with no authority. Capacity to order anyone to do anything is virtually nonexistent. Hence, you have to build relationships, connect to the target, and get the target to "want to do" what it should do anyway.

Self-management You yourself are your first direct report. But whether you have yourself, alone, or several other direct reports, you essentially have three foci: the job, the assignments within the job, and overseeing completion of the assignments.

Social fabric A socially connective and cohesive workplace is a creative and productive one, because there is a substrate of social interaction in the organization. A job place, by contrast, is one where you arrive, do business, and leave. A workplace is where jobs, tasks, and work intermingle to some extent and there is a feeling of camaraderie and community.

Span of control and communication In the span of control, administrators can supervise five employees. In the span of communication, they can resource 50 because they do not have to check the work of each staff member; that person checks his or her own work and seeks help if and as needed.

Staffing One of the key managerial competencies that comprise PSOSBPE. Staffing identifies people needed to accomplish a task. It answers the question "Who?" Who will we need for this project, and when? What skill mix will we need? Staffing involves recruiting, onboarding, training, supervising, directing, training, educating, coaching, evaluating, and motivating.

Strategic plan Strategic plan provides the basis for the annual plan that an organization's executive director carries out. The board of directors should ensure that such a plan is in place and that it is connected to the evaluation of the executive director.

Supervisor The first step on the organizational staircase. Supervisors oversee employees more frequently than tasks or projects. Responsible for assisting one or more persons in doing their jobs—on time and according to law and policy. Supervisors have five task bundles: professional, managerial, supportive, developmental, and reflective.

Tasks Comprised of parts and elements. People, equipment, and jobs intersect at tasks. Task bundles are assembled in batches and then combined in a string of tasks. When completed, they result in an organization's product.

Task-project orchestration Orchestration is the process through which tasks coalesce into projects and are completed. Projects involve a range of people and competencies. They must be "orchestrated," and the manager must know the "score"—the external factors/events outside their projects—and must synchronize order, sequence, tempo, entrances and exits of parts, and elements so the outcome is on time and on budget.

Teams Groups organized around achievement or completion of specific jobs, tasks, and other initiatives. Examples include the governance team, the C-level team, and the middle management team.

Temperament A "default" style of interacting with ourselves and others, one's temperament is one's core. Sense of temperament enables a person to be operationally aware of when its display is appropriate and to experiment with adopting other temperaments/styles.

Temporary coping mechanisms These are small practices that can be implemented during the course of a day to help manage and mitigate stress on a daily basis. Recharging, gathering strength, and collecting focus throughout the day is key to keeping stress from accumulating and escalating.

Terminal derailment Precipitating behaviors that are immediate cause for dismissal. These include ethical breeches, betrayal of trust, specific behavioral problems, substance abuse, and uncollegial attitudes.

Time management and leadership Time management and leadership refers to prioritization and schedule control. It is nothing more (or less) than a time budget that controls the amount of time spent on an item. Time budgets are crucial in work that lacks natural temporal boundaries.

Wicked problem Social or cultural problem of indeterminate scope or scale that is difficult or impossible to solve. Its insolubility may stem from incomplete or contradictory knowledge, number of people and opinions involved, large economic burden, or interconnected nature of wicked and other problems.

Work A set of projects that, as they are collectively successful, accomplish the mission of the organization and embody and articulate its raison d'etre or purpose. It embodies the organization's core values in such a way that the goals are produced via acceptable means. Effective leaders organize, catalyze, and synthesize work into efficient, effective products and services.

Abrams, J. (1990). Tips from the Menninger Clinic and mental fitness strategies. *Compass,* November, 72–74.

Baken, J. (2005). *The corporation: The pathological pursuit of profit and power.* New York, NY: Free Press.

Blanchard, K. (1999). *The one-minute manager balances work and life.* New York, NY: William Morrow.

Blanchard, K. H., Edington, D. W., & Blanchard, M. (1986). *The one minute manager gets fit* (1st ed.). New York, NY: William Morrow.

Bock, L. (2015). *Work rules! Insights from inside Google that will transform how you live and lead* (1st ed.). London, U.K.: John Murrary.

Bossidy, L., Charan, R., & Burck, C. (2002). *Execution: The discipline of getting things done* (1st ed.). New York, NY: Crown Business.

Bradford, D., & Cohen, A. (1997). *Managing for excellence.* Hoboken, NJ: Wiley.

Bramson, R. M. (1981). *Coping with difficult people* (1st ed.). Garden City, NY: Anchor Press/Doubleday.

Bramson, R. M. (1992). *Coping with difficult bosses.* New York, NY: Carol.

Bridges, W. (2004). *Transitions: Making sense of life's changes* (2nd ed.). Cambridge, MA: Da Capo Press.

Buckingham, M. (1999). *First break all the rules: What the world's greatest managers do differently.* New York, NY: Simon & Schuster.

Budd, J. (n.d.). *The evolution of HRM* [Video]. Coursera. Retrieved from www.coursera.org/learn/managing-human-resources/lecture/clClQ/video-the-historical-evolution-of-hrm

Bustin, G. (2014). *Accountability: The key to driving a high-performance culture.* New York, NY: McGraw-Hill Education.

Carver, J. (2006). *Boards that make a difference.* San Francisco, CA: Jossey-Bass.

Chamorro-Premuzik, T. (2019). *Why do so many incompetent men become leaders?* Cambridge: Harvard Business Review Press. Retrieved from https://hbr.org/2013/08/why-do-so-many-incompetent-men

CliftonStrengths Assessment. (n.d.). www.gallupstrengthscenter.com

Collins, J. C. (n.d.). Concepts: The Hedgehog concept. Retrieved from https://www.jimcollins.com/concepts/the-hedgehog-concept.html

Conger, R. (2017). *You go first: Become the leader your team needs.* Eagle, ID: Aloha.

CreativeHRM.com. (n.d.). History of human resources management. Retrieved from http://www.creativehrm.com/hr-management-history.html

Darling, M., Parry, C., & Moore, J. (2005, July 1). Learning in the thick of it. Retrieved from https://hbr.org/2005/07/learning-in-the-thick-of-it

Davidson, W. (2015). *Business writing: What works, what won't.* New York, NY: St. Martin's Griffin.

DeGraff, J. T., & DeGraff, S. (2017). *The innovation code: The creative power of constructive conflict* (1st ed.). Oakland, CA: Berrett-Koehler.

Dotlich, D., Noel, J., & Walker, N. (2004). *Leadership passages: The personal and professional transitions that make or break a leader.* San Francisco, CA: Jossey-Bass.

Ferazzi, K. (2009). *Who's got your back.* New York, NY: Crown Business.

Flesch, R. (1996). *The classic guide to better writing.* New York, NY: Collins Reference.

Freiler, L. (n.d.). Alpha vs. beta testing. Retrieved from https://www.centercode.com/blog/2011/01/alpha-vs-beta-testing/

Gallary, C. (2014). Sharpening vs. honing. Retrieved from www.thekitchn.com/did-you-know-this-steel-doesnt-actually-sharpen-knives-211855

Gallo, C. (2014). *Talk like Ted: The 9 public-speaking secrets of the world's top minds.* New York, NY: St. Martin's Press.

Gebelein, S., et al. (2010). *The successful managers handbook: Develop yourself, coach others* (8th ed.). Los Angeles, CA: Korn Ferry Leadership Consulting.

Goysberg, B., Lee, J., Price, J., & Cheng, J. Y.-J. (2018, January 1). The culture factor. *Harvard Business Review.* Retrieved from https://hbr.org/2018/01/the-culture-factor

Grant, A. (2014). *Give and take: Why helping others drives our success.* New York, NY: Penguin Books.

Hill, A., Mellon A., & Goddard, J. (2018, September 27). *How winning organizations last 100 years.* Cambridge: Harvard Business Review Press. Retrieved from https://hbr.org/2018/09/how-winning-organizations-last-100-years

Huber, A. (2018). *Telling the design story: Effective and engaging communication.* New York, NY: Routledge.

International Bottled Water Association. (2015). Market industry report. Retrieved from http://www.bottledwater.org/public/BWR_Jul-Aug_2016_BMC%202015%20bottled%20water%20stat%20article.pdf#overlay-context=economics/industry-statistics

Janis, I. L., & Mann, L. (1977). *Decision making: A psychological analysis of conflict, choice, and commitment.* New York, NY: Free Press.

Kegan, R., & Lahey, L. L. (2001). *How the way we talk can change the way we work: Seven languages for transformation* (1st ed.). San Francisco, CA: Jossey-Bass.

Kehoe, D. (n.d.). Effective communication skills. *The Great Courses.* www.thegreatcourses.com

Leap Ambassadors. (2016). The performance imperative. Retrieved from https://leapambassadors.org/products/performance-imperative/

Lepore, J. (2009, October 5). Not so fast. *The New Yorker.* Retrieved from https://www.newyorker.com/magazine/2009/10/12/not-so-fast

Logic Model Development Guide. (n.d.). www.wkkf.org/resource-directory/resource/2006/02/wk-kellogg-foundation-logic-model-development-guide

Lombardo, M., & Barnfield, H. (2014). *FYI: For your improvement—Competencies development guide* (6th ed.). Minneapolis,MN: Korn Ferry.

Lubit, R. (2003). *Coping with toxic managers, subordinates and other difficult people: Using emotional intelligence to survive and prosper.* Upper Saddle River, NJ: FT Prentice Hall.

Lyons, S., & Kuron, L. (2013). Generational differences in the workplace: A review of the evidence and directions for future research. *Journal of Organizational Behavior, 35,* S139–S157. doi/10.1002/job.1913/full

Manfred, F. R., de Vries, K., & Miller, D. (1991). *The neurotic organization: Diagnosing and revitalizing unhealthy companies.* New York, NY: HarperCollins.

Marciano, P. (2010). *Carrots and sticks don't work.* New York, NY: McGraw-Hill Education.

Menninger Clinic. (n.d.). Professionals program. Retrieved from www.menningerclinic. com/patients/professionals-in-crisis-program

MindTools.com. (n.d.). Smart goals: How to make your goals achievable. Retrieved from www.mindtools.com/pages/article/smart-goals.htm

Morgan, J. (2014). *The future of work: Attract new talent, build better leaders, and create a competitive organization.* Hoboken, NJ: Wiley.

Myers, G. C. & Holusha, J. (1986). *When it hits the fan: Managing the nine crises of business.* New York, NY: Houghton Mifflin Harcourt.

Myers, G. C. & Holusha, J. (1986). *When it hits the fan: Managing the nine crises of business.* New York, NY: Houghton Mifflin Harcourt.

Naisbitt, D., & Naisbitt, J. (2018). *Mastering megatrends: Understanding & leveraging the evolving new world.* Hackensack, NJ: World Scientific.

Naisbitt, J. (1984). *Megatrends: Ten new directions transforming our lives.* New York, NY: Warner Books.

Pinola, M. (2013). How to make PowerPoint Presentations amazing. Retrieved from https://lifehacker.com/how-can-i-make-my-powerpoint-presentations-amazing-507552122

Psych Central. (n.d.). What is emotional intelligence (EQ)? Retrieved from https:// psychcentral.com/lib/what-is-emotional-intelligence-eq/

Schmidt, E. (2017, December 6). Rediagnosing founder's syndrome: Moving beyond stereotypes to improve nonprofit performance. *Nonprofit Quarterly.* Retrieved from https://nonprofitquarterly.org/2017/12/06/rediagnosing-founder-s-syndrome-moving-beyond-stereotypes-to-improve-nonprofit-performance/

Schwartz, T. (n.d.). *The way we work podcast with John Hope Bryant.* Retrieved from https://theenergyproject.com/podcasts/episode-two-john-hope-bryant/

SimpleDollar.com. (2007). Review: *What Got You Here Won't Get You There.* Retrieved from www.thesimpledollar.com/review-what-got-you-here-wont-get-you-there/

SmartDraw Flowchart Symbols. (n.d.). Retrieved from www.smartdraw.com/flowchart/ flowchart-symbols.htm

Society for Implementation Research. (n.d.). Home. Retrieved from https://societyforim plementationresearchcollaboration.org/

Snow, D., & Yanovitch, T. (2009). *Unleashing excellence: The complete guide to ultimate customer service* (2nd ed.). Hoboken, NJ: Wiley.

Sostrin, J. (2013). *Beyond the job description: How managers and employees can navigate the true demands of the job.* New York, NY: Palgrave Macmillan.

Stone Motes, P., & McCartt Hess, P. (2007). *Collaborating with community-based organizations through consultation and technical assistance.* New York, NY: Columbia University Press.

Sutton, R. (2012). *Good Boss, bad boss.* New York, NY: Business Plus.

Sutton, R. (2017). *The asshole survival guide.* New York, NY: Houghton Mifflin Harcourt.

TEDx Talks. (n.d.). *Music paradigm: Roger Nierenberg at TEDxRiversideAvondale.* Retrieved from https://www.youtube.com/watch?v=QE8Sj_nggp0

TenHaken, V. (2016). *Lessons from Century Club companies: Managing for long-term success* (1st ed.). Ann Arbor, MI: Spinner Press.

TheEnergyProject.com. (n.d.). What's your capacity gap? Retrieved from https://theenergyproject.com

Tropman, J. E. (1984). *Policy management and leadership and the human services.* New York, NY: Columbia University Press.

Tropman, J. E. (1998). *Does America hate the poor?* New York, NY: Praeger.

Tropman, J. E. (1998). *The management of ideas in the creating organization.* Westport, CT: Quorum Books.

Tropman, J. E. (2003). *Making meetings work: Achieving high-quality group decisions.* Thousand Oaks, CA: SAGE.

Tropman, J. E. (2017). *Team impact.* San Diego, CA: Cognella Academic.

Tropman, J. E., & Harvey, T. J. (2013). *Nonprofit governance: The why, what, and how of nonprofit boardship* (updated edition). Chicago, IL: ACTA.

Truity.com. (n.d.) The typefinder (research edition). Retrieved from https://www.truity.com/test/type-finder-research-edition

Vaill, P. B. (1982). The purpose of high-performing systems. *Organizational Dynamics, 11,* 23–29.

VCU Libraries Social Welfare History Project. (n.d.). Freedmen's Bureau. Retrieved from https://socialwelfare.library.vcu.edu/federal/freedmen's-bureau/

Weiss, L. (2018). *How we work.* New York, NY: HarperCollins.

What Google learned from its quest to build the perfect team. (2016, February 28). *The New York Times Magazine.* Retrieved from www.nytimes.com/2016/02/28/magazine/what-google-learned-from-its-quest-to-build-the-perfect-team.html

White, P. (2015). Five signs that your workplace may be toxic. Retrieved from www.fastcompany.com/3045927/5-signs-that-your-workplace-may-be-toxic

Zoller, K. & Preston, K. (2014). *Enhancing your executive edge: How to develop the skills to lead and succeed.* New York, NY: McGraw-Hill Education.

REFERENCES

Accounting Aid Society.com. (n.d.). About us. Retrieved from http://accountingaidsociety. org/about-us/

Argyris, C. (1985). *Strategy, change, and defensive routines*. Boston, MA: Pitman.

Benedict, R. (1934). *Patterns of culture*. Boston, MA: Houghton Mifflin.

BoardSource.com. (n.d.). Support for boards. Retrieved from https://boardsource.org/ board-support/

Bohlman, L. G., & Deal, T. E. (2003). *Reframing organizations: Artistry, choice, and leadership* (3rd ed.). San Francisco, CA: Jossey-Bass.

Bridges, W. (2004). *Transitions: Making sense of life's changes* (2nd ed.). Cambridge, MA: Da Capo Press.

Business 101: Principles of Management. (n.d). Chapter 5: Organizational change. Lesson 5: Lewin's 3-stage model of change. Retrieved from https://study.com/ academy/course/principles-of-management-course.html

Carey, B. (2004, June 22). Fear in the workplace: The bullying boss. *The New York Times*.

Cherry, K. (2017). www.verywell.com/what-is-emotional-intelligence-2795423.

Cohen, E. A., & Gooch, J. (1990). *Military misfortunes: The anatomy of failure in war*. New York, NY: Free Press.

Cohen, M. D., March, J. G., & Olsen, J. P. (1972). A garbage can model of organizational choice. *Administrative Science Quarterly, 17*, 1–25.

Collins, J. C. (2001). *Good to great: Why some companies make the leap—and others don't* (1st ed.). New York, NY: Harper Business.

Collins, J. C. (2005). *Good to great and the social sectors*. New York, NY: Harper Business.

Covey, S. R. (1990). *The seven habits of highly effective people: restoring the character ethic* (1st Fireside ed.). New York, NY: Fireside Book.

Crutchfield, L. R., & McLeod Grant, H. (2008). *Forces for good: The six practices of high-impact nonprofits* (1st ed.). San Francisco, CA: Jossey-Bass.

Deming, W. E. (1986). *Out of the crisis*. Cambridge, MA: Massachusetts Institute of Technology, Center for Advanced Engineering Study.

Dempsey, R., & Chavous, J. M. (2013). Commander's intent and concept of operations, *Military Review*. Retrieved from http://usacac.army.mil/CAC2/MilitaryReview/ Archives/English/MilitaryReview_20131231_art011.pdf

DeSmet, Name. (1992, July 10). City merchants' anti-panhandling campaign raises an issue of morality. *Detroit News*.

de Vries, M. F. R., & Miller, D. (1984). *The neurotic organization* (1st ed.). San Francisco, CA: Jossey-Bass.

Douglas, E. (1998). *Straight talk: Turning communication upside down for strategic results at work* (1st ed.). Palo Alto, CA: Davies-Black.

Du Bois, W. (1901). The Freedmen's Bureau. *The Atlantic, 87*(519). https://www. theatlantic.com/magazine/archive/1901/03/the-freedmens-bureau/308772/

Fernández-Aráoz, Roscoe, C. A., & Aramaki, K. (2018, September-October). From curious to competent. *Harvard Business Review.*

Frumkin, P. (2002). *On being nonprofit: A conceptual and policy primer.* Cambridge, MA: Harvard University Press.

Garvin, D. A. (2013, December). How Google sold its engineers on management. *Harvard Business Review.*

Gawande, A. (2011, September 26). The coach in the operating room. *The New Yorker.* Retrieved from https://www.newyorker.com/magazine/2011/10/03/personal-best

Goldsmith, M. (2007). *What got you here won't get you there.* New York, NY: Hyperion.

Goleman, D. (1995). *Emotional intelligence.* New York, NY: Bantam Books.

Half, R. (2017, April 28). The secrets to hiring and managing Gen Z. Retrieved from https://www.roberthalf.com/research-and-insights/workplace-research/the-secrets-to-hiring-and-managing-gen-z

Harvey, J. B. (1974). Abilene paradox. *Organizational Dynamics, 3,* 63–80.

Hensler, P. (2012, December 1). The equilibrium of collective wrongness or the effect of mindfulness on advisor performance after market dislocations. Retrieved from http://digital.case.edu/concern/texts/ksl:weaedm402

Hensler, P. A. (2011, December 1). The effect of organizational and individual learning from disruptive market events on financial advisor behavior. Retrieved from http://digital.case.edu/concern/texts/ksl:weaedm401

Hirschman, A. O. (2004). *Exit, voice, and loyalty: Responses to decline in firms, organizations, and states.* Cambridge MA: Harvard University Press.

Hochschild, A. R. (2012, 1983). *The managed heart: Commercialization of human feeling.* Berkeley: University of California Press.

Hochschild, A. R., & Machung, A. (1989). *The second shift: Working parents and the revolution at home.* New York, NY: Viking.

Hodson, R. (2001). *Dignity at work.* New York, NY: Cambridge University Press.

Independent Sector. (2016). Principles of good governance and ethical practice. Retrieved from www.independentsector.org/resource/principles-preview/

Janis, I. L. (1983). *Groupthink: Psychological studies of policy decisions and fiascoes* (2nd rev. ed.). Boston, MA: Houghton Mifflin.

Janis, I. L., & Mann, L. (1977). *Decision making: A psychological analysis of conflict, choice, and commitment.* New York, NY: Free Press.

Kanter, R. (1982). *The change masters.* New York, NY: Simon & Schuster.

Kerr, S. (1975). On the folly of rewarding A, While hoping for B. *Academy of Management Journal, 18*(4), 769–783. https://doi.org/10.5465/255378

Kidder, T. (1981). *The soul of a new machine* (1st ed.). Boston, MA: Little, Brown.

Koestler, A. (1964). *The act of creation.* London, U.K.: Hutchinson.

Kogon, K., Wood, J., & Blakemore, S. (2015). *Project management for the unofficial project manager.* Dallas, TX: Ben Bella Books.

Lipman, V. (2017, January 25). How to manage generational differences in the workplace. *Forbes*. Retrieved from https://www.forbes.com/sites/victorlipman/2017/01/25/how-to-manage-generational-differences-in-the-workplace/

March, J. G., & Simon, H. (1958). *Organizations*. New York, NY: Wiley.

McCaskey, M. B. (1982). *The executive challenge: Managing change and ambiguity*. Boston, MA: Pitman.

McKay, A. (Dir.). (2015). *The big short*. https://www.imdb.com/title/tt1596363/?ref_=nv_sr_1

McMaster, H. R. (1997). *Dereliction of duty: Lyndon Johnson, Robert McNamara, the joint chiefs of staff, and the lies that led to Vietnam* (1st ed.). New York, NY: HarperCollins.

McMaster, H. R. (2005.) Memorandum for squadron and troop commanders. Subject: Concept of the operations headquarters, 3d Armored Cavalry Regiment.

Merton, R. K. (1957). *Social structure and process*. Glencoe, IL: Free Press.

Michalko, M. (2012, March 3). What monkeys teach us about the assumptions we make, *The Creativity Post*.

Mintzberg, M. (2007, 1989.) *Mintzberg on management: Inside our strange world of organizations*. New York, NY: Free Press.

Myers, G. C., & Holusha, J. (1986). *When it hits the fan: Managing the nine crises of business*. New York, NY: Houghton Mifflin Harcourt.

Myers-Briggs Foundation. (n.d.). MTBI basics. Retrieved from https://www.myersbriggs.org/my-mbti-personality-type/mbti-basics/home.htm?bhcp=1

Network for Social Work Management, Human Services Management Competencies. (n.d.). www.socialworkmanager.org NCCS Data Archive. (n.d.). Retrieved from http://nccs-data.urban.org/index.php

O'Loughlin, M. (2017). Pope Francis says give to the homeless. *American Magazine*. Retrieved from www.americamagazine.org/politics-society/2017/02/28/pope-francis-says-give-homeless-dont-worry-about-how-they-spend-it-lent

Parsons, T. (1960). Some ingredients of a general theory of formal organization. In *Structure and process in modern societies*. Glencoe IL: Free Press.

Peter, L., & Hull, R. (2011). *The Peter principle: Why things always go wrong*. New York, NY: Harper Business.

Peters, T. (1988). Restoring American competitiveness: Looking for new models of organizations. *Academy of Management Executives, 2*, 103–107.

Peters, T. J., & Waterman, R. H. (1982). *In search of excellence: Lessons from America's best-run companies* (1st ed.). New York, NY: Harper & Row.

Portney, S. (2017, 2000). *Project management for dummies* (5th ed.). Hoboken, NJ: Wiley.

Quinn, R. E. (1988). *Beyond rational management: Mastering the paradoxes and competing demands of high performance* (1st ed.). San Francisco, CA: Jossey-Bass.

Rittel, Horst W. J. (1973). Dilemmas in a general theory of planning. *Policy Sciences, 4*, 155.

Rozovsky, J. (2016). ReWork. Retrieved from https://rework.withgoogle.com/blog/five-keys-to-a-successful-google-team/

Sandberg, S. (2014, January 17). How do we cultivate women leaders? NPR. Retrieved from https://www.npr.org/2014/01/17/261090111/how-do-we-cultivate-women-leaders

Sayles, L. R., & Chandler, M. K. (1971). *Managing large systems: Organizations for the future*. New York, NY: Harper & Row.

Schwantes, M. (2017). How do you know if you work for a toxic manager? They will do any of these 8 things daily. *Inc.com*. Retrieved from www.inc.com/marcel-schwantes/ how-do-you-know-you-work-for-a-toxic-manager-they-will-do-any-of-these-10-things-daily.html

Schwartz, T. (n.d.). *The way we work podcast with John Hope Bryant*. Retrieved from https://theenergyproject.com/podcasts/episode-two-john-hope-bryant/

Scott, A. O. (2004, June 30). Film review: Giving corporations the psychoanalytic treatment. *The New York Times*. Retrieved from www.nytimes.com/2004/06/30/movies/ film-review-giving-corporations-the-psychoanalytic-treatment.html

Siegel, D. J., & Bryson, T. P. (2018). *The yes brain: How to cultivate courage, curiosity, and resilience in your child* (1st ed.). New York, NY: Bantam.

Solomon, M. (2002). *Working with difficult people*. Paramus, NJ: Prentice Hall.

Star Thrower Distribution. (n.d.). *More than one right answer with Dewitt Jones*. Retrieved from https://www.youtube.com/watch?v=YI-9tuMg1s8

Sullivan, P. (2017, December 21). New year, old-fashioned investment strategy. *The New York Times*. Retrieved from www.nytimes.com/2016/01/09/your-money/new-year-old-fashioned-investment-strategy.html

Tannen, D. (1990). *You just don't understand: Women and men in conversation* (1st ed.). New York, NY: William Morrow.

The Flat Earth Society. (n.d.). Retrieved from https://www.tfes.org/

Thomas, W. I., & Thomas, D. S. T. (1928). *The child in America: Behavior problems and programs*. New York, NY: Alfred A. Knopf.

Thurber, J. (1945). *The Thurber carnival*. New York, NY: Harper.

Tichy, N. M., & Devanna, M. A. (1986). *The transformational leader*. New York, NY: Wiley.

Tolbize, A. (2008). *Generational differences in the workplace*. St. Paul: University of Minnesota, Research and Training Center on Community Living. Retrieved from https://rtc3.umn.edu/docs/2_18_Gen_diff_workplace.pdf

Tropman, J. E. (1984). *Policy management and leadership and the human services*. New York, NY: Columbia University Press.

Tropman, J. E. (1986). *Conflict in culture: Permission versus control in alcohol use in American society*. Lanham, MD: University Press of America.

Tropman, J. E. (2001). *The compensation solution: How to develop an employee-driven rewards system*. San Francisco, CA: Jossey-Bass.

Tropman, J. E., & Richards-Schuster, K. (2000). The concept of system levels in social work. In P. Allen-Meares & C. Garvin (Eds.), *The handbook of social work direct practice* (pp. 65–84) Thousand Oaks, CA: SAGE.

Tropman, J. E., & Schaefer, H. L. (2004). *Title*. Location: Publisher.

Tuchman, B. (1985). *The march of folly: From Troy to Vietnam*. New York, NY: Random House.

Tufte, E. (1990). *Envisioning information*. Cheshire, CT: Graphics Press.

University of Michigan. (2018). MHealthy Program. Retrieved from https://hr.umich.edu/benefits-wellness/health-well-being/mhealthy/more-mhealthy/about-mhealthy/mhealthys-overview-mission

Vaill, P. B. (1982). The purpose of high-performing systems. *Organizational Dynamics, 11*, 23–29.

Vidich, A. J., & Bensman, J. (1958). *Small town in mass society.* Princeton NJ: Princeton University Press.

Weber, M. (1946). *Essays in sociology.* New York, NY: Oxford University Press.

Weiss, L. (2018). *How we work.* New York, NY: HarperCollins.

Whetten, D. A., & Cameron, K. S. (2015). *Developing managerial skill* (9th ed.). New York, NY: Pearson.

White, P. (2015). Five signs that your workplace may be toxic. Retrieved from www.fastcompany.com/3045927/5-signs-that-your-workplace-may-be-toxic

INDEX

Tables and figures are indicated by *t* and *f* following the page number

For the benefit of digital users, indexed terms that span two pages (e.g., 52–53) may, on occasion, appear on only one of those pages.